JUNK

FURNITURE ReFRESHED

Beautiful

30 Clever FURNITURE Projects to Transform Your Home

SUE WHITNEY
Founder of JUNKMARKET Style

Photography by Douglas E. Smith

The Taunton Press

Text © 2017 Sue Whitney
Photographs © 2017 Douglas E. Smith

 **The Taunton Press**
Inspiration for hands-on living®

The Taunton Press, Inc., 63 South Main Street, PO Box 5506, Newtown, CT 06470-5506
Email:tp@taunton.com

Editor: Carolyn Mandarano
Copy Editor: Betty Christiansen
Indexer: Heidi Blough
Art Director: Rosalind Loeb Wanke
Jacket/Cover design: Sandra Salamony
Interior design and layout: Sandra Salamony
Photographer: Douglas E. Smith

The following names/manufacturers appearing in *Junk Beautiful: Furniture ReFreshed* are trademarks: A&W®, Anchor Hocking®, Annie Sloan Chalk Paint®, Armour Etch®, Behr®, Benjamin Moore®, CrossFit®, DeWalt®, Fitbit®, Gorilla®, Habitat for Humanity® ReStore®, Haeger® Potteries, iPad®, J-B® Weld,Kreg®, Krylon® Looking Glass®, Lift Off®, Loctite® Naval Jelly®, Martha Stewart Crafts®, Minwax® Polycrylic™, Mod Podge®, Penetrol®, Real Milk Paint® Ultra Bond, Rust-Oleum® Chalked Paint, Rust-Oleum® Chalked Protective Topcoat, Rust-Oleum® Universal® Hammered Spray Paint, Speed® Square, Speedo®, TinkerToy®, Tough Mudder®, Valspar®, X-Acto®, Zep®, Zinsser® B-I-N®

Library of Congress Cataloging-in-Publication Data

Names: Whitney, Sue, author.
Title: Junk beautiful furniture refreshed : 30 clever furniture projects to
   transform your home / Sue Whitney.
Description: Newtown, CT : The Taunton Press, Inc., 2017.
Identifiers: LCCN 2017012781 | ISBN 9781631868375
Subjects: LCSH: Furniture finishing. | Used furniture. | Salvage (Waste,
   etc.) in interior decoration.
Classification: LCC TT199.4 .W47 2017 | DDC 749–dc23
LC record available at https://lccn.loc.gov/2017012781

Printed in the United States of America
10 9 8 7 6 5 4 3 2 1

ABOUT YOUR SAFETY: Working wood is inherently dangerous. Using hand or power tools improperly or ignoring safety practices can lead to permanent injury or even death. Don't try to perform operations you learn about here (or elsewhere) unless you're certain they are safe for you. If something about an operation doesn't feel right, don't do it. Look for another way. We want you to enjoy the craft, so please keep safety foremost in your mind whenever you're working.

ACKNOWLEDGMENTS

To begin, I would like to thank one very special person who has been by my side through the making of every publication. Doug Smith is not only my photographer but also a true creative partner. Thanks from the bottom of my heart ZWL from your gal pal LGY. To my longtime besties, Lanette, Marge, Sharon, Dianne, and Janell, who gave of themselves and their homes, I am eternally grateful. Last, but certainly not least, a heartfelt thanks to my brothers, Howard and Rich, and their lovely brides, Barbara and Gretchen, for their unwavering love and support. Love all of you lots.

I took up residence in a tiny Minnesota river town to generate the book and am appreciative for the kindness of the folks and business owners of Lanesboro, Minnesota, and surrounding areas. The studio provided by Barb from E2 Boutique made possible many of the magical images. The ladies of Community Grounds shared their building on more than one occasion. Brad, Elaine, and Shanalee of Beautiful Something were there for anything needed, from vintage wares to hauling, and even my wardrobe needs! Gordy and Val, owners of several businesses, also covered my tail on a variety of fronts. Then there is Skip Schwartz, the man behind the scenes, who hauled my projects and props from point A to point B and back again for six long months! Cheers! My studio was a bustling place, so on occasion I needed a respite from the madness. Kudos to Pat of Grandma's Inn and Patrick from Iron Horse Outfitters and Inn for providing several much-needed reprieves!

Other chief supporters include the many fine dealers from Generations of Harmony Antique Mall, Melissa Klema of Adourn, and Four Daughters Vineyard & Winery. The folks at Generations provided an endless supply of very cool vintage and antique props for the book as well as some of the inspirational pieces for the actual projects. The talented Melissa of Adourn also provided inspiration and allowed us access to her lovely home and shop for photography sessions. Four Daughters shared their stunning venue for several photography sessions, including the cover!

Other appreciated cohorts who played key roles in the success of this book include Brian Quail of ReFind Works, Dave and Naomi Atkinson of Tin Treasures, Kim Flicek of Joyful Revival, and the Coyle family. Thanks to everyone for having my back!

Hugs,

DEDI-CATION

Sending encouragement to all women who have endured domestic abuse. Stay strong ladies!

CONTENTS

FOREWORD: SALVAGE STYLE RESURGENCE 2
FOREWORD: REVIVING VINTAGE TREASURES 4
INTRODUCTION 6
LET'S TALK PICKIN' 9

THE GATEWAY TO YOUR HOME 40
BASIC YET COOL STORAGE PIECES

STUFF COAT HANGER 41
BOOT TRAY 46
CHILD'S BENCH 50

KITCHEN CAPERS 55
FUN AND FUNCTIONAL GALLEY GOODS

WHITE BREAKFAST TABLE 56
FLATWARE BOX–CUM–CHARGING STATION 62
CHALKBOARD AND EASEL 70
KITCHEN WINDOW HERB GARDEN 76

EAT, DRINK & BE MERRY 80
DINING ROOM DIGS

MODERN DINING TABLE AND CHAIRS 81
ARCHITECTURAL SALAD SERVER 88
INTENTIONAL CRACKLE GLAZE SIDEBOARD 94

SKIP TO MY LOO 101
BREATHTAKING BATHROOM
FURNITURE AND STORAGE

CRAFTY CURIO CONVERSION 102
RUSTIC TOWEL BAR 108
LADDERBACK CHAIR BATHROOM CADDY 112

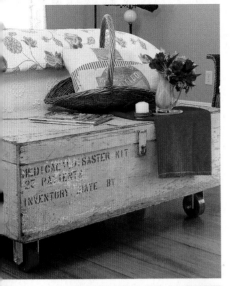

GATHER ROUND 116
INVITING PIECES FOR INSPIRED
GATHERING ROOMS

DEWALT GAME TABLE 117
MODERN COFFEE TABLE 124
LADDER BAR 130

THE LIVING IS EASY 136
CASUAL AND COMFORTABLE FURNISHINGS

MEDICAL STAND BLANKET HOLDER 137
ROOM DIVIDER 142
WICKER BASKET TABLE 148

BED CHAMBERS 152
SLEEPING QUARTERS DÉCOR

BOHEMIAN BED 153
LUMINESCENT NIGHTLIGHT 160
ROLL-AROUND BLANKET CHEST 164
ART DECO DESK 170

RETREAT AND RESTORE 177
MAKEOVERS FOR GETAWAY SPACES

ROLL-ABOUT DESK 178
MODERN DESK CHAIR 184
VELVETEEN CHAIR REBORN 188
REFRESHED RATTAN PATIO SET 193

RESOURCES 199
INDEX 200

SALVAGE STYLE RESURGENCE

—DON TAYLOR SHORT, Owner of West End Architectural Salvage and host of DIY Network's *West End Salvage*

Sue Whitney is the original "junkmaster" in the vintage, salvage, and re-style industry. She is an unabashed designer and continually offers an avant-garde vision to do-it-yourselfers, vintage enthusiasts, and those of us who make our wage in the industry.

As a visionary, Sue has been taking risks, opening new doors, and inspiring all since the inception of JUNKMARKET. Sue's new book, *Junk Beautiful: Furniture ReFreshed*, showcases her uncanny ability to forge new paths and stay well ahead of the curve when it comes to innovative creations for your home by employing her "style without borders" approach. *Junk Beautiful: Furniture ReFreshed* will be as comfortable on your coffee table as it will be in your workshop.

In 2000, I was in the business of renovating and rehabbing classic homes. I used vintage and salvaged items and was able to restore neglected homes to their original splendor. At the end of each project, I was left with a wide array of salvaged items and soon found my storage unit overflowing with vintage treasures. I hosted a two-week tag sale in 2005 to get rid of the pieces. To my amazement, the sale was so successful that customers returned weekend after weekend and my salvage business was born. In 2008, I moved West End Architectural Salvage into our current 50,000-sq.-ft. warehouse on the edge of downtown Des Moines. There (along with my talented team) I restore, design, build, and sell custom furniture, artwork, and any and all pieces of architectural salvage. After two successful seasons of the popular HGTV/DIY network television series *West End Salvage*, we find ourselves happily serving customers throughout the United States.

I had the pleasure of meeting Sue Whitney in my store in 2007 when she was working on her first book. Sue and I have built a lasting friendship while enjoying many adventures in the worlds of DIY, handcrafted, repurposed, salvage, vintage, and antiques. Whether we find ourselves at West End or at one of Sue's occasional art and vintage markets, we have fun sharing our vision and concepts for the future of the ever-changing marketplace. As leading style-makers, we continue to offer inspiration and guidance to all ages and aptitudes while meeting the wide variety of style preferences of our customers. Through projects and design concepts that adhere to the "three P rule"—pretty, practical, and plausible—Sue continues to be a trendsetter. Throughout the pages of this new book, Sue consistently hits the vintage nail on the head!

There is a definite surge in salvage style in our industry, due largely to the do-it-yourself trend. Online resources like Etsy and Pinterest have actively engaged a more youthful audience particularly in the areas of DIY, handmade, furniture restoration, and vintage design. Customers of all ages are walking into West End with an insatiable appetite for all that is unique. They are in search of one-of-a-kind furnishings and accessories that tell a story and help create a unique home environment. The renaissance of folks who want to be hands-on is also prevalent in our current marketplace. Many of our customers

There is wide appeal in taking a vintage piece, applying some creativity and a hands-on approach, and making it your own.

walk in and see our items as the beginning of a new project. There is wide appeal in taking a vintage piece, applying some creativity and a hands-on approach, and making it your own. We constantly listen to customer needs, stay abreast of industry trends, and honor the tradition of our vintage pieces. This is a recipe for success in the world of vintage.

Sue Whitney clearly understands and shares my beliefs in constantly pushing the refresh button in our industry and consistently offers distinctive concepts, practical solutions, and impeccable style for each and every one of her followers. I can't wait to start dog earring my copy of *Junk Beautiful: Furniture ReFreshed* in my workshop.

REVIVING VINTAGE TREASURES

—DR. LORI VERDERAME, director of DrLoriV.com and History Channel expert

*J*unk Beautiful: Furniture ReFreshed demonstrates Sue Whitney's unquestioned prowess in the realm of vintage furniture repurposing and design.

As a Ph.D. antiques appraiser and History Channel expert, I evaluate more than 20,000 objects every year—much of it vintage furniture—from audiences the world over. When it comes to old furnishings, I know value when I see it. *Junk Beautiful: Furniture ReFreshed* is an inspiration to those who love vintage furnishings, enjoy DIY projects, and want to bring historic treasures home. Sue's unique approach to repurposing vintage objects as well as interior design makes this book a must-read.

Sue and I have a relationship that spans decades. We have shared the stage at events held worldwide, and we also share a love of art, antiques, and collectibles. Sue has spent her career making a silk purse out of a sow's ear in the repurposing arena, while I have saved valuable, rare antiques from the Dumpster. In front of large and enthusiastic

audiences, online, and on TV, radio, and social media, Sue has demonstrated how to breathe new life into old stuff. Over the years, Sue has remained dedicated to reviving aging treasures and sharing her creative spirit and unmatched skills to renew pieces that others might have relegated to the trash pile. In *Junk Beautiful: Furniture ReFreshed*, Sue highlights repurposing projects and interior designs that focus on modern forms, clean lines, and real-life functionality. In short, Sue shows us how revisiting midcentury modernism is all the rage when it comes to repurposing projects and interior design.

When you repurpose, refinish, or refresh a piece, it becomes your own. And when an aging piece is refreshed by your own hand, it celebrates your history as well as your handiwork.

Furniture pieces that multitask are necessities within today's 21st-century lifestyle. It is furniture that helps make a house a home. When you repurpose, refinish, or refresh a piece, it becomes your own. Using Sue's tips and room decorating ideas in *Junk Beautiful: Furniture ReFreshed*, you can reconsider that flea market find or revive Grandma's Victorian settee and give it a fresh, new, contemporary feel. When an aging piece is refreshed by your own hand, it celebrates your history as well as your handiwork. *Junk Beautiful: Furniture ReFreshed* not only shares Sue's innovative ideas and tried-and-true repurposing techniques, but it also sparks the urge to repurpose those aging pieces and make them stand out in your home.

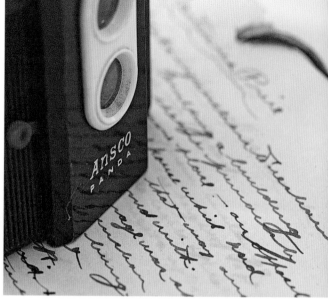

INTRODUCTION

Book number four. Wow! I am pleased to have yet another JUNK Beautiful opportunity to share my passion with you. Thanks to all who have followed and supported me throughout the past two decades. The road has taken me in many different directions, and I have learned much from my adventures and the gifted people I have met along the way. What I see on the horizon for the future of vintage décor is exciting, and throughout this book, you'll witness an insurgent change of course that embodies the evolution of JUNKMARKET Style.

I launched JUNKMARKET in 2000, with its main objective to emerge as the leading style maker in the vintage décor industry. It took off like wildfire, identifying with the demand in the interior design field. My vision from the beginning was to instill timeless creative strategies for home improvement and home décor through the use of reclaimed, repurposed, and vintage furnishings and accessories. I remain committed to the original JUNKMARKET mission but recognize a need for renewal. A trailblazer must lead, not follow. A new generation of junkers has emerged, and I am forging pioneering paths that will energize the youth yet embolden those of us who have been around the block.

Learn from those you taught. My daughter Elizabeth, as a member of the "captive audience" in my home, had no choice than to live by the JUNKMARKET rule. Now that she has come of age, I am in awe of how she truly embraced the concept and has developed her own contemporary view on the subject. She is an inspiration and always keeps me on my toes by encouraging me to continue to step outside my happy place and remain original and up-to-date in the ever-changing world of vintage.

This book addresses the needs of youthful newbies, vintage veterans, and everyone in between. Be sure to read through Let's Talk Pickin', starting on p. 10. Some will view this basics section as a first-timer's DIY tool, while others will use it as a refresher course. The projects that line the pages are diverse, high quality, quick, and easy, making them approachable for everyone.

What's really refreshing? The clean, contemporary book design and propping for the photography, which represent my "style without borders" approach and less-is-more philosophy. I hope you will find the projects themselves and the manner in which they are interpreted to be refreshingly forward thinking. Until next time.

See you on the junk pile!

Sue

LET'S TALK PICKIN'!

SHOP 'TIL YOU DROP

TOOLS AND MATERIALS TO REFRESH YOUR FINDS

JUNKER'S TOOLBOX
· Project: Tool Time Caddy

PAINTER'S TOOLBOX
· Paint Finishes
· A Word on Whites
· Project: Paint-by-Numbers Storage

WOOD AND METAL FINISHER'S TOOLBOX

CRAFTER'S TOOLBOX
· Project: Organ Pipe Art Supply Shelf

SAFETY FIRST KIT

LET'S TALK PICKIN'!

The world of vintage furniture and accessories is constantly evolving. What's old is new, is new again, and vintage décor is experiencing a resurgence thanks to the younger set, who are updating the look with a contemporary flair. I like to call this clean and modernized approach to vintage design "style without borders."

The latest advances inside the vintage movement give new meaning to the phrase *thinking outside the box*. Looks like urban industrial, rustic modern, vintage prairie, and contemporary cottage—or the combination of any of these—are blazing new trails in vintage décor.

The "style without borders" approach is not only for the young and hip new crowd, but also for the young at heart. Junkers and vintage enthusiasts who have been pickin' for years are embracing the new frontier with unbridled enthusiasm. You'll find this fresh approach to vintage well represented in the ingenious projects included in this book. You could just jump right in to refreshing your favorite finds, but I would recommend spending some quality time reading through this chapter first. Although freedom of expression is the ultimate goal, there are time-tested guidelines, tips, and tricks of the trade that provide the necessary tools for success.

SHOP 'TIL YOU DROP

If you love to go junking, there's one thing you need to keep in mind before heading out:

Plan on hauling away heavy pieces of furniture, awkward oddities, fragile architectural pieces, and rusty farm implements. In preparation for the experience, don't miss your workout, arm yourself with tools of the hauling trade, dress appropriately, and drive the right rig! Now that you are fully primed, let's talk about places that are ripe for the picking.

If you are looking for value and selection, **flea markets** are an obvious choice. They vary in size and assortment, so do your fact checking to see which of the venues in your area is right for you. Bear in mind that most fleas are rain-or-shine events, and inclement weather makes a notable difference in attendance by dealers and shoppers alike. For the best values, I like to shop in the rain. Go figure! Remember, flea markets are simply a place to get the goods and typically don't offer "style" settings or decorating ideas.

Small-town **antique malls** are one of my preferred places to pick. They normally have an ample number of dealers who offer a wide variety of products from bigs to smalls. Antique malls are oftentimes staffed by the dealers, who are as knowledgeable about

other vendors' inventory as they are about their own. This is very helpful when you are in search of something particular. Prices will vary, but even if you are an ardent junker, you will find cool things in your price range.

Barn sales, vintage and art shows, and pop-ups are also excellent resources. I prefer the intimate to midsize shows in these genres, as it is extremely difficult to properly curate vendors at a mega show. Small to mid-size shows and sales are easier to navigate, provide better opportunities to develop relationships with dealers, and facilitate smart buying over impulse purchases.

Occasional sales are another shopping option ripe for the picking. These are either single-shop events or community collaborations. Occasionals, as they are known, are typically held on a select number of weekends per year. Oftentimes they are themed for the season so the shopper will know what to expect when it comes to the vintage items on hand for purchase. A newer version of the occasional sale is popping up around the country. People are actually doing themed sales right out of their own homes. Fun stuff!

There are so many places to shop, I simply can't name them all. Other notables (and some of my favorites) include architectural and regular salvage stores, junk shops, used-restaurant-supply stores, Goodwill, Salvation Army Thrift Stores, city cleanups, tag sales, and community garage sales. A good old-fashioned summertime drive down country roads is also not a bad way to go. You never know what you might find!

JUNKER'S TOOLBOX

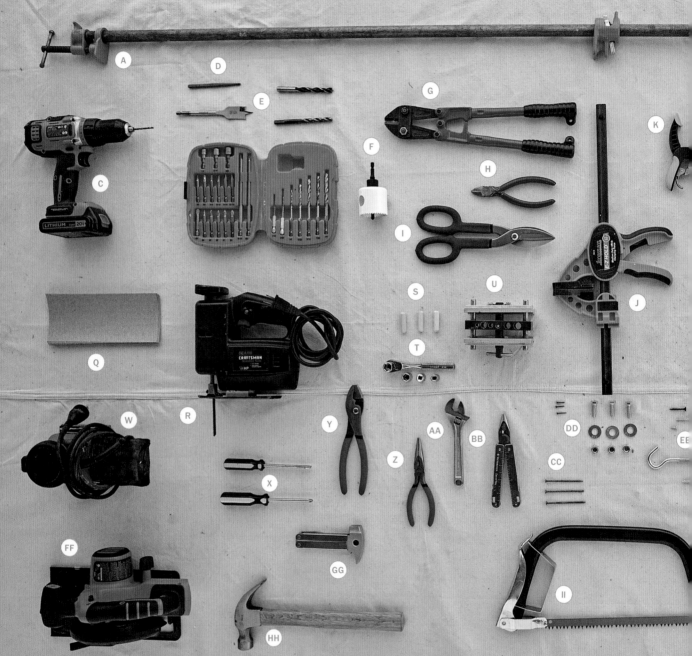

A. pipe clamp
B. carpenter square
C. power drill
D. metal punch
E. a variety of drill bits including a spade bit, and metal and wood drill bits
F. hole saw
G. bolt cutter
H. wire cutter
I. tin snips
J. bar clamp
K. spring clamp
L. measuring tape
M. D-ring hangers
N. picture hanging wire
O. gorilla wall hangers
P. Speed® Square
Q. sandpaper
R. power jigsaw
S. dowels pins
T. socket wrench and standard socket set
U. dowel jig
V. marking pencil
W. power sander
X. Phillips and flat-head screwdrivers

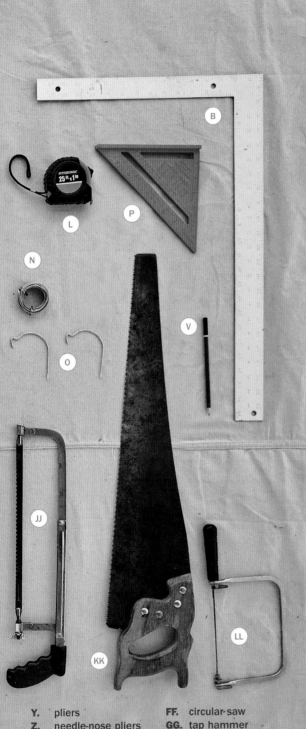

Make the Tool Time Caddy project on p. 26 to store your tools.

TOOLS AND MATERIALS TO REFRESH YOUR FINDS

The following sections will bring you up to speed on everything you will need to create the projects found in this book and many projects you will imagine and construct on your own. I'm introducing you to just the basic building blocks of tools and materials used when refreshing furniture, but you will be surprised at the level of sophistication you can achieve with these basics. As you become more experienced, you can invest in more high-tech tools. One step at a time!

Remember, the junk items used in my projects may be one-of-a-kind items. The instructions, tools, and materials for my projects only refer to how I refreshed and transformed the junk I found. You may need to improvise to achieve your desired transformation . . . and chances are, your projects will look even better. Let's get started!

JUNKER'S TOOLBOX

The Junker's Toolbox contains the basic tools and hardware you will need to get started as a weekend warrior. These are all good investment pieces for novices as well as more experienced builders and refinishers. All tools in the toolbox have been used in the projects contained in the book. If there is a specialty tool or piece of hardware used in a specific project, it will be called out in that project's "Tools Needed" section.

Y.   pliers
Z.   needle-nose pliers
AA. wrench
BB. multipurpose tool
CC. variety of nails
DD. nuts, bolts, screws, and washers
EE. Hook bolt and nuts, and eye hook
FF. circular-saw
GG. tap hammer
HH. hammer
II.   bow saw
JJ. hacksaw
KK. handsaw
LL. coping saw

PAINTER'S TOOLBOX

A.	paint tray	**F.**	sample-size latex	**L.**	Krylon® Looking	**R.**	Real Milk Paint®	**U.**	Rust-Oleum
B.	paint roller with		paint		Glass® spray		Ultra Bond		automotive
	a variety of roller	**G.**	chalk-based paint		paint	**S.**	Rust-Oleum®		spray paint
	pads	**H.**	quart-size latex	**M.**	crackle glaze		Universal®	**V.**	paint stripper
C.	straight and		paint		finish		Hammered Spray	**W.**	putty knife
	angled latex	**I.**	milk paint	**N.**	shop rags		Paint	**X.**	stain-blocking
	paintbrushes	**J.**	paint pan	**O.**	art brushes	**T.**	Krylon spray paint		primer
D.	chip brushes	**K.**	paint remover	**P.**	stir sticks			**Y.**	paint-measuring
E.	sponge brushes			**Q.**	painter's tape				container

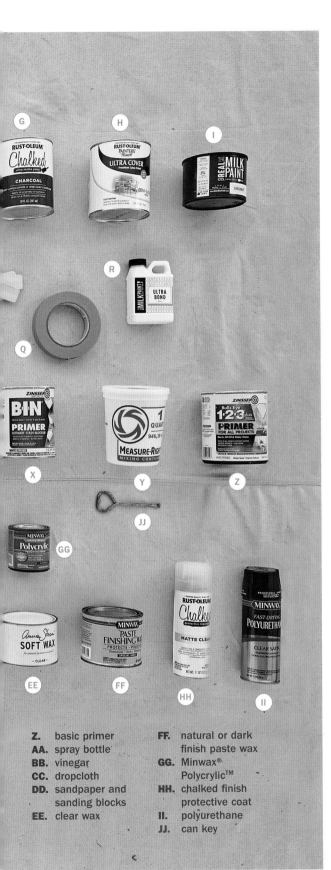

Make the Paint-by-Numbers file cabinet project on p. 30 to store your paints and supplies.

PAINTER'S TOOLBOX

Let the fun begin! Painting is not the only way to refresh your furniture finds, but in many cases, it can be the best option for offering your treasures a new lease on life. Paint products currently on the market are endless, and choosing a product can seem a bit overwhelming. Throughout this book, I will present different paint finishes to clear up some of the confusion on when to use what product.

But selecting the proper paint is not the only important detail when painting furniture. Having all of the necessary tools at hand is also essential to getting the job done right.

PAINT FINISHES

Most people think that the easiest way to refresh a piece of furniture or an accessory is with paint. While that might be true, you can't just throw on any kind of paint and expect the piece to be exactly what you wanted. For me, it's all about options.

Before the obsession with milk paint products and chalk-based paints began, there was latex. Although milk and chalk-based paints are great alternatives for furniture, that doesn't mean latex no longer has a home in the furniture-painting arena. It most certainly does. As you will find in the projects, latex can provide an assortment of finishes other than old world, antique, or vintage, which is generally your end result with the other two options. Latex has four main sheens to choose from, and all can be utilized in different applications when painting furniture.

Z. basic primer
AA. spray bottle
BB. vinegar
CC. dropcloth
DD. sandpaper and sanding blocks
EE. clear wax
FF. natural or dark finish paste wax
GG. Minwax® Polycrylic™
HH. chalked finish protective coat
II. polyurethane
JJ. can key

Flat latex, also known as matte, has the least sheen of the four types of paint, as it does not reflect light. It is the best selection for hiding imperfections or covering rough surfaces, but keep in mind that it is far less durable than the other sheens and difficult to clean. If you are using flat as your main paint, you may want to consider applying a protective finish over the paint, such as a matte finish poly-urethane or Rust-Oleum Chalked Protective Topcoat, matte clear. Flat latex is not the best choice for furniture that will be heavily used or placed in high-traffic areas.

Satin latex, also referred to as eggshell, has more luster than flat, but it is not shiny. It has a velvety, almost pearl-like appearance when dry. It will resist stains better than a flat and can be wiped clean. A piece painted with a satin finish can be placed in rooms that have some exposure to moisture and can withstand moderate use. I would recommend applying a protective coat such as Minwax polyurethane in a clear satin finish.

Semi-gloss latex is a much tougher finish than satin, making it a better option for furniture that will be placed in high-traffic areas or subjected to more abuse through use. It is a bit shiny, as it reflects more light than a satin finish. It will stand up better to water and cleaning than either a flat or satin. If you want to achieve a clean, more modern finish on your piece of furniture, semi-gloss latex is an excellent choice. You do not need to apply a topcoat over semi-gloss latex, but if you wish to, Minwax polyurethane in a semi-gloss finish or Minwax Polycrylic are good options.

Gloss latex produces a hard, shiny finish. It is the toughest finish of the four, and furniture painted with gloss can typically withstand a ton of wear and tear, making it the best option for high-traffic rooms in your home. If you're after a glamorous finish such as piano black, gloss is your answer. Some will say you can't get a piano finish with water-based latex, but I disagree! If the gloss paint is applied properly, and you use a topcoat of either Minwax gloss clear polyurethane or Minwax Polycrylic, you can achieve a hard, shiny, and beautiful piano-like finish.

I steer clear of oil-based paint and use only latex when painting furniture. Oil-based paint is slowly being regulated out by the government—it has more odor, it's more difficult to use, and cleanup is a nightmare. Latex may not be as durable as oil-based paint, but it is more environmentally friendly and far less complicated to work with.

Stain can also be employed when creating paint finishes with latex. If you want a more vintage or antique feel, you can achieve this look with latex paint by distressing and waxing prior to applying a protective coat.

SAFETY FIRST KIT

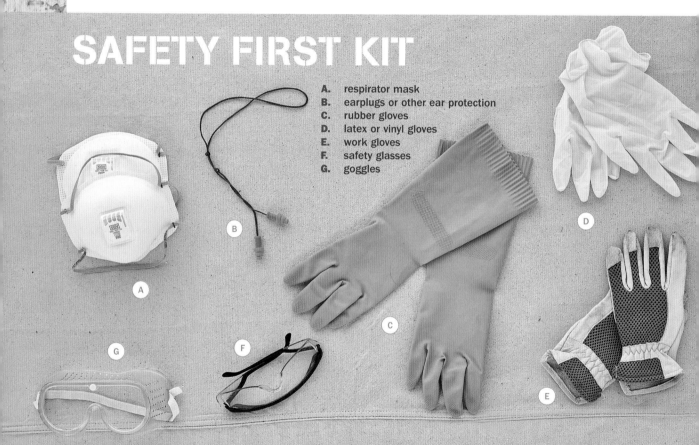

A. respirator mask
B. earplugs or other ear protection
C. rubber gloves
D. latex or vinyl gloves
E. work gloves
F. safety glasses
G. goggles

Please, always remember to be safe! Working with tools and chemicals can be dangerous business, so the need to educate yourself about what you are using is imperative. All products on the market come with manufacturer's instructions and warning labels. Before tackling your job, take the time to read through this information carefully. Follow all directions to a T because they are there for a reason. If you have further questions or concerns after reading a warning label, contact the manufacturer directly or do online research.

Have all your safety equipment ready at hand and in good working condition. Keep in mind that chemical warning labels not only instruct you on how to work safely with the product, but also on how to store it properly when not in use. I know I sound like your mother, but I care about your health and well-being!

A WORD ON WHITES

Oh, the wonderful world of whites. I say that with tongue in cheek, as we all know how difficult choosing the right white can be. White in the paint world is rarely white. Tricky little undertones are to blame for our dilemma with the color. The undertones are intended to deliver personality, and that they do! Knowing what their personality might be is another question. For example, blue and silver undertones tend to proffer a brighter, more contemporary white while yellow and gold will produce a soft, buttery white. Most hardware and paint stores have broken down their white selections into undertone categories. This is very useful. If you are still having difficulty, speak with one of the paint specialists on staff. These folks are very helpful and can even supply you with the formula of the colors you are considering.

The best tip, however, is to research the white selections online. It's nothing short of amazing. You think you are looking at colors when you view the white palettes online, but you are looking at white. What comes across crystal clear online are the undertones as the white fades away into the background. Another thing you should keep in mind is that colors, including whites, appear different under different lighting situations. Always paint a sample on your selected piece and live with it in your room of choice for several days to make sure you have a chance to see it under all lighting conditions.

My final rule of thumb on the subject is simple. Choose a few white colors you love and stick with them. It's very hard to make a mistake that way. As you know, I am inspired by vintage pieces, so I have selected four stunning vintage vessels that inspired my whites of choice. Enjoy!

Pure white. I chose this lovely vintage Vitrock white glass vase to represent a pure white. Anchor Hocking® produced Vitrock during the latter part of the Depression. This glass is an opaque solid white. The most common undertone color for a pure white is blue. Other undertones may include gray and silver. If you are looking for the purest of pure, choose one with as little undertone as possible.

I like pure white for furnishings in bathrooms and kitchens because it is clean and bright. Whites with other undertones can tend to look dirty in these rooms. Some examples of pure whites are Decorators White by Benjamin Moore®, Ultra Pure White by Behr®, and Ultra White by Valspar®.

Grayed-down white. This beautiful white ironstone china piece is an ideal example of a vintage grayed-down white. Ironstone is a glaze-covered earthenware that was first patented in England by Charles James Mason in 1813. His patent was short-lived, so other companies followed suit. Gray and white are my two favorite colors, so what could be better than white with gray undertones? Slight purple undertones may also produce a similar shade.

Refreshed furniture of white with traces of gray can also work nicely in the bathroom or kitchen, but I find this shade ideal for restful rooms such as the bedroom. Experience has taught me that graying down any color adds a softness that is very soothing. Statuesque by Behr, White from Benjamin Moore, and Valspar's Sandstone are a few of the grayish whites I am drawn to.

Buttery white. A soft, buttery white is a natural selection for a vintage home. Yellow and gold undertones will produce this yummy white. My go-to vintage pottery pick is a clean-lined pair of Royal Haeger vases. Other than the pottery itself, I love the fact that the company Haeger® Potteries was based in Kane County, Illinois, home to one of my favorite places to pick, the Kane County Flea Market.

Buttery whites work well in many rooms in your home. Pieces created for your living quarters or dining room would be lovely done up in this shade. Ivory Dust from Valspar, Linen White by Behr, and Benjamin Moore's Linen White are colors reflective of Royal Haeger pottery.

Antique white. The warmth of a more antique or off-white is always a welcome addition to a vintage-inspired abode. My muse for this color is a midcentury Brush flower bowl. The Brush Pottery Company was established in 1925 after a stint as the Brush-McCoy Pottery Company. This has caused some confusion between Brush and Nelson McCoy pieces. The undertones found in this pottery are more likely browns, but gold or orange may produce a similar shade. Be careful when choosing an orange undertone, as it may come off as peachy under some lights.

I would not choose this color for the bath or kitchen, but you can use it in most other spaces in your home. Polished Pearl by Behr, Benjamin Moore's Sail Cloth, and Homestead Resort Cameo White from Valspar are a few colors worth checking out.

WOOD AND METAL FINISHER'S TOOLBOX

A. Sunnyside TSP Substitute cleaner	**I.** rust-removing block	**P.** construction adhesive	**W.** scratch-correction pencils	**EE.** Howard Feed-N-Wax® special dark paste wax
B. bleach	**J.** tack cloth	**Q.** J-B® Weld	**X.** gel stains	**FF.** paste finishing wax
C. dish soap	**K.** spray degreaser	**R.** epoxy	**Y.** penetrating stain	
D. vinegar	**L.** artist's brush	**S.** cutting oil	**Z.** Minwax Polycrylic	**GG.** paste wax
E. wood filler	**M.** wood glue	**T.** Penetrol®	**AA.** chip brush	**HH.** variety of sandpapers
F. shop rags	**N.** Gorilla® Super Glue	**U.** Loctite® Naval Jelly®	**BB.** black tea	
G. putty knife	**O.** wood weld	**V.** staining pads	**CC.** steel wool	
H. sanding blocks			**DD.** polyurethane	

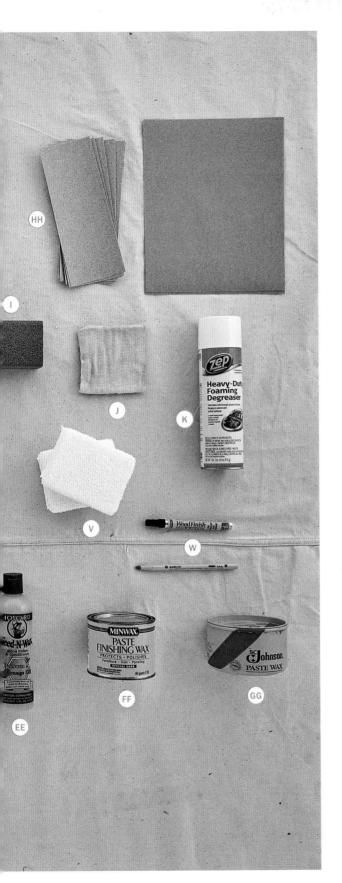

WOOD AND METAL FINISHER'S TOOLBOX

Some pieces of furniture are better restored without the use of paint. Just because paint exists doesn't make it appropriate in every case. In fact, paint in some cases may destroy the value of a piece. If you don't know what you have in your hands, do the research before you refresh in any way. Natural woods and metals are gorgeous even if some blemishes are present. In my world, we call that character! In this book, I reintroduce some forgotten old-school methods as well as introduce new and wonderful products on the market.

CRAFTER'S TOOLBOX

A.	fabric	**H.**	electric staple gun	**N.**	ribbon
B.	variety of needles	**I.**	hot-glue gun and glue stick	**O.**	buttons
C.	embroidery thread	**J.**	cloth measuring tape	**P.**	colored pencils
D.	paper cutter	**K.**	lace trim	**Q.**	chalk pencil
E.	straightedge	**L.**	iron-on fabric adhesive	**R.**	pencil sharpener
F.	sandpaper and sanding block	**M.**	hem tape	**S.**	charcoal pencil
G.	staples			**T.**	X-Acto® knife

- **A.** fabric
- **B.** variety of needles
- **C.** embroidery thread
- **D.** paper cutter
- **E.** straightedge
- **F.** sandpaper and sanding block
- **G.** staples
- **H.** electric staple gun
- **I.** hot-glue gun and glue stick
- **J.** cloth measuring tape
- **K.** lace trim
- **L.** iron-on fabric adhesive
- **M.** hem tape
- **N.** ribbon
- **O.** buttons
- **P.** colored pencils
- **Q.** chalk pencil
- **R.** pencil sharpener
- **S.** charcoal pencil
- **T.** X-Acto® knife
- **U.** box cutter
- **V.** scissors
- **W.** wire cutter
- **X.** hole punch
- **Y.** wood embellishments
- **Z.** sand
- **AA.** large rocks
- **BB.** moss
- **CC.** small stones
- **DD.** stencil
- **EE.** solid craft paper
- **FF.** patterned craft paper
- **GG.** shelf liner
- **HH.** chalk pen
- **II.** paint pen
- **JJ.** sponge brush
- **KK.** chip brush
- **LL.** stencil brush
- **MM.** various art brushes

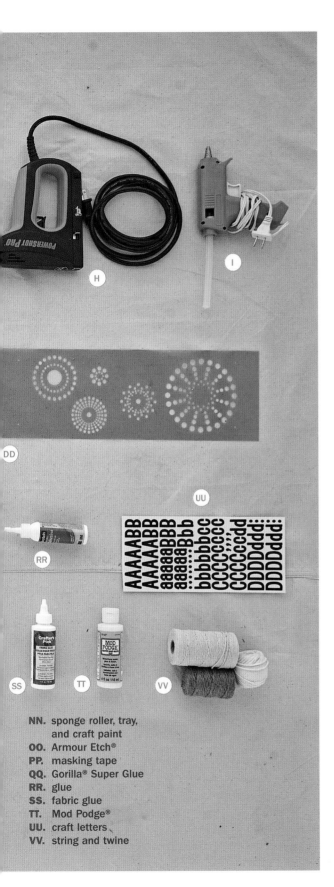

NN. sponge roller, tray, and craft paint
OO. Armour Etch®
PP. masking tape
QQ. Gorilla® Super Glue
RR. glue
SS. fabric glue
TT. Mod Podge®
UU. craft letters
VV. string and twine

KNOW HOW

Even if you are not a crafter, keeping a small stash of crafting items on hand will allow for more creative freedom.

Make the Organ Pipe Art Supply Shelf project on p. 34 to store your crafts.

CRAFTER'S TOOLBOX

Craft products play a vital role in furniture and accessory re-dos. As Doug (my partner-in-crime photographer) and I would say, craft supplies help put the "general prettiness" in a project. Textiles, papers, and naturals are great materials to add texture and softness to a refreshed furnishing, while artsy embellishments can offer up a just-right finishing touch. Don't be afraid to add detail to a piece by picking from your craft stash. It's a great way to add some personality just before you cross the finish line.

JUNKER'S TOOLBOX PROJECT

TOOL TIME CADDY

I was indeed fortunate to find a sturdy, handcrafted reclaimed barn-board tabletop with no legs. This is not an everyday occurrence. I knew that it would take just a few simple alterations to make it a hardworking yet attractive tool caddy.

BOTTOMS UP

Have I told you yet that I like to flip things upside down? If not, I do. Now that we have that understood, I encourage you to look at your vintage finds with an open mind. Not everything has to be as it appears. When I discovered this beautifully crafted tabletop, I was immediately drawn to the bottom and its grayed-down barn board. I knew I could stain the new frame a dark brown to play off the deep gray palette of the weathered wood. Also, the real tabletop didn't make sense to me. It was rough and uneven, making it difficult to set for dinner, much less keep your wineglass from spilling.

Who says your garage can't look fabulous? Just because something is utilitarian doesn't mean it should be lacking in style.

After making the decision to turn the bottom up, my wheels were set in motion. The raised frame provided ideal space to hang the tools from, leaving the barn board to shine on undisturbed in all its natural glory. What a great get!

THE BOLD AND THE BEAUTIFUL

Reclaimed barn board is rustic in nature, but the elements I chose to supplement the rugged tabletop are not. The contrast between weathered and modern makes a bold and beautiful design statement. The bright red colors of the accessories help to further define the statement. My goal was to create an eye-catching piece that was practical in nature. The well-designed and sturdy build of the tabletop combined with industrial trappings of the trade solved my quest for practicality.

To enhance the tool caddy, I brought in a small but mighty old bench and some vintage wood vises that are as useful today as when they were constructed. You know what they say: Vintage birds of a feather fly together. Overall, this is a rough-and-tumble garage great!

ABOVE RIGHT I've been dying to try one of these gadgets, and my tool caddy gave me the opportunity. I don't get out much!

RIGHT I'm a huge fan of broom clips as they have many uses. Red ones are even better.

TOOL TIME CADDY

I love recovering projects that are already half done for me when I find them. There's nothing wrong with salvaging an item left undone. I was not sure what I would do with this tabletop when I found it, but I knew it had extraordinary possibility for repurpose. I surprised myself with the outcome!

MATERIALS NEEDED

- Wood and Metal Finisher's Toolbox (see p. 22)
- Painter's Toolbox (see p. 14)
- Abandoned tabletop
- 2 magnetic tool strips
- 6 broom clips
- Twenty ³⁄₈-in. Kreg® pocket hole plugs
- Five 4-in. wood letters
- Black flat latex paint

TOOLS NEEDED

- Junker's Toolbox (see p. 12)
- Safety First Kit (see p. 18)

METHOD

1. Clean the bottom and top of the tabletop with a rag and warm, soapy water.

2. Apply wood glue to the inside of the pocket holes (which existed on the salvaged tabletop) and insert pocket hole plugs. **A** Allow to dry.

3. Sand the surface of the tabletop bottom frame. Wipe away all sanding residue with a tack cloth.

4. Using a staining pad, apply gel stain to the tabletop bottom frame and allow to dry. **B** Apply polyurethane to the bottom and top of the tabletop and allow to dry.

5. Measure and mark the top of the tabletop for 2 D-ring hangers. This is now the back of the project. Drill pilot holes and attach D-ring hangers where marked.

6. Flip the tabletop back to the bottom side. Measure and mark for the magnetic tool strips. Drill pilot holes and attach both magnetic strips. **C**

7. Measure and mark for 6 broom clips. Drill pilot holes where marked and attach each of the broom clips.

8. Paint each of the letters with black latex paint. Allow to dry.

9. Measure and mark for the placement of the letters. Drill pilot holes and attach where marked. I used 2 decking screws per letter.

PAINTER'S TOOLBOX PROJECT

PAINT-BY-NUMBERS STORAGE

Let's face facts. Storage is a battle that needs a suitable solution. My friend had a shed for storing her paint and supplies, but nothing really to store the stuff in other than the shed itself. Her paint-by-number artwork collection was all the fodder I needed to get the party started!

WHIMSICAL STORAGE

Sometimes it's a good thing to take a walk on the whimsical and wacky side of the road! Even if you have a more conservative edge to your day-to-day design style, it's fun to pick a spot where anything goes. A heated shed that's just for her is one such spot where you can run amok. No one has anything to say about it but you! I adored the happy camper cottage appeal of the shed and set out to select something that would play off its charm. It's hard to believe that the disgustingly dirty file cabinet I rescued from a truck bed would work, but I knew by its bones it had excellent potential for the job at hand.

The worst part about salvaging the critter was removing all of the grit, grease, and grime along with the textured paint job that must have been done some time in the '70s. The answer was a spray degreaser. I just sprayed it on and watched my cares melt away.

The little she side of this shed was perfect for my file cabinet to hold all painting odds and ends.

Know when something isn't worth salvaging. The outward appearance of my file cabinet gave me pause, so I gave it a once-over for sturdiness.

ABOVE Paintbrushes, the most essential tool for painting, get the top-drawer position.

RIGHT I topped off the cabinet with art brushes in jars and a pair of vintage brushes for good measure.

FAR RIGHT Organization was the main objective for my file cabinet. There were enough drawers to put everything needed in proper categories. Make things easier on yourself by labeling the drawers in a fashion that makes sense to you.

PAINT-BY-NUMBERS STORAGE

Late-night shopping is the best! While scanning the streets of a closed-for-the-evening flea market, I picked this right out of a dealer's truck before he headed home. It's not just any file cabinet. The drawers have a very unusual configuration, and that's what makes this piece stand out in a crowd.

MATERIALS NEEDED

- Painter's Toolbox (see p. 14)
- Crafter's Toolbox (see p. 24)
- Old file cabinet
- White satin latex paint
- Blue satin latex paint
- Paint chips

TOOLS NEEDED

- Junker's Toolbox (see p. 12)
- Safety First Kit (see p. 18)

METHOD

1. Remove the drawers from the cabinet, then clean all surfaces with a rag and warm, soapy water. Wearing gloves and a mask, apply Howard Feed-N-Wax to the drawers with a shop rag, then apply Minwax Polycrylic to the drawers. **A** Set the drawers aside.

2. Apply Zep® degreaser to the painted wood surfaces of the file cabinet. Following the manufacturer's instructions, allow it to soak in, then wipe it off with a shop rag. **B**

3. With a clean rag, wipe all degreased surfaces with warm water. Gently sand the surfaces to scrape off any raised grain.

4. Apply paint primer to the sanded surfaces. Let dry, then paint the frame of the cabinet with white satin latex paint. Let dry.

5. Tape off the side panels and paint the inside of the panels with blue satin latex paint. **C** Let dry. Apply chalked protective topcoat to all painted surfaces.

6. Lay decorative paper inside the drawers and crease with a straightedge. Cut the paper using a straightedge and box cutter. Using the paper as a guide, measure and cut the shelf liner to size and insert it into the drawers. **D**

7. Measure and cut paint chips to fit the label holder pulls. Adhere letters based on how you will organize your drawers. Insert the paint chip labels into the holders.

ONCE UPON A PIPE

ORGAN PIPE ART SUPPLY SHELF

Believe it or not, my craft room organizer is constructed primarily of orphan organ pipes. I find them by the dozens and have used them in a wide variety of projects. They are so beautiful in their own right simply as art, but sturdy construction also makes them ideal fodder for this organizing shelf.

GO WITH THE FLOW

Most of us have certain predispositions for vintage goods. These are the penchants from which we draw inspiration in our individual artistic processes. If all the juice came from the same orange, the world would be a dull place. Just sayin'.

I've long admired organ pipes. I'm drawn to these musical ditties because they are carefully constructed, made from gorgeous wood, of modern design, and boast abundant detail. The combination of these attributes set my once-upon-a-pipe vision in motion. This shelf was not my initial concept for the pipes. The instruments were earmarked for one project and the paintbrushes for another. I randomly set the two together, and the lightbulb turned on. Allow yourself the leeway for derailment. If you permit yourself to change course, magical and delightful things are bound to happen.

Birds of a feather flock together to engineer this matchless craft tools coordinator that will address any creative space woes.

KNOW HOW

This piece can double as tabletop art. Forget the hooks and flip it upside down. It resembles a big-city skyline in an abstract way.

ABOVE LEFT Copper wire is as eye-catching as it is industrious. I reclaimed mine from a construction site. Old tarnished paintbrushes are highly sought after. Showcase your collection in an artful way.

ABOVE When possible, I keep the original markings intact on my junk subject, showing its true identity.

LEFT Storing supplies in supplies is a space saver on a small shelf. Look for vintage or used pottery, twine, and string as storage elements. Or pick up some restaurant pottery at a used-restaurant-supply store and use those containers to stow supplies, too.

ORGAN PIPE ART SUPPLY SHELF

Getting organized is one thing, but staying organized is quite another. Make it easier on yourself by creating something pretty to look at. I call this the "spoonful of sugar" method for orderliness. Give it a go and make Mary Poppins proud!

MATERIALS NEEDED

- Wood and Metal Finisher's Toolbox (see p. 22)
- 5 vintage organ pipes of varying sizes
- Dark brown gel stain
- Gray liquid stain
- 12-in. flat bar, 1/16 in. thick
- 24-in. by 8-in. laminate shelf
- 2 cup hooks
- 5 vintage paintbrushes
- Copper wire

TOOLS NEEDED

- Junker's Toolbox (see p. 12)
- Safety First Kit (see p. 18)
- Countersink drill bit

METHOD

1. Sand the organ pipes with fine- to medium-grit sandpaper. Use a power sander on the flat sections and switch to sandpaper or a block to get into tight spots.

2. Wearing gloves and a mask, wash all surfaces with Sunnyside TSP Substitute, then wipe them clean with a shop rag and warm, soapy water. Let dry.

3. Apply epoxy to the insides of the organ pipes and clamp together. Measure and attach the flat bar to the back of the pipes with decking screws. Put 2 screws in the back of each pipe to secure. If your flat bar is not predrilled, drill pilot holes first. **A**

4. Apply the gel stain, then cover with liquid stain before the gel stain dries. **B** This will add a nice patina. Allow to dry thoroughly.

5. Center the organ pipes on the shelf and mark with painter's tape. Drill 2 pilot holes in the top of the organ pipes and 2 pilot holes in the bottom of the shelf on either side of the center line. Line up the holes, then attach the shelf to the organ pipes with a countersink drill bit. **C**

6. Measure and mark the back of the organ pipes for hanging wire. Screw in two 2½-in. wood screws partway, wrap with hanging wire, and tighten the screws.

7. Measure and mark the bottom of the shelf for the cup hooks, centering them between the end of the shelf and the pipes. Drill pilot holes and screw in the cup hooks.

8. Hammer 2 tacks partway into each organ pipe, place 1 brush in between, and wrap copper wire around the tacks to secure the brush. Do this with the other 4 brushes. I like to leave a bit of wire at the end and form it into a curlicue. **D**

FURNITURE & ACCESSORY PROJECTS

THE GATEWAY TO YOUR HOME
BASIC YET COOL STORAGE PIECES
- Stuff Coat Hanger
- Boot Tray
- Child's Bench

KITCHEN CAPERS
FUN AND FUNCTIONAL GALLEY GOODS

- White Breakfast Table
- Flatware Box–cum–Charging Station
- Chalkboard and Easel
- Kitchen Window Herb Garden

EAT, DRINK & BE MERRY
DINING ROOM DIGS
- Modern Dining Table and Chairs
- Architectural Salad Server
- International Crackle Glaze Sideboard

SKIP TO MY LOO
BREATHTAKING BATHROOM FURNITURE AND STORAGE
- Crafty Curio Conversion
- Rustic Towel Bar
- Ladderback Chair Bathroom Caddy

GATHER ROUND
INVITING PIECES FOR INSPIRED GATHERING ROOMS
- DeWalt Game Table
- Modern Coffee Table
- Ladder Bar

THE LIVING IS EASY
CASUAL AND COMFORTABLE FURNISHINGS
- Medical Stand Blanket Holder
- Room Divider
- Wicker Basket Table

BED CHAMBERS
SLEEPING QUARTERS DÉCOR
- Bohemian Bed
- Luminescent Nightlight
- Roll-Around Blanket Chest
- Art Deco Desk

RETREAT AND RESTORE
MAKEOVERS FOR GETAWAY SPACES
- Roll-About Desk
- Modern Desk Chair
- Velveteen Chair Reborn
- Refreshed Rattan Patio Set

THE GATEWAY TO YOUR HOME

BASIC YET COOL STORAGE PIECES

Nothing says "welcome home" like the gateway to your abode. There's much to consider when designing projects for your entryway, but I believe the main objective is to keep your gear corralled in a tidy yet attractive fashion. No one wants to come home after a long day to be greeted by a disorderly space that just means more work before play. The trick to managing the mess is to get the whole family to participate in your cut-the-clutter campaign. Clever interpretations of classic entryway essentials might convince your clan to keep it clean!

GOT STUFF?

STUFF COAT HANGER

It's time to talk about fun stuff! I had a "pot of gold" encounter when I came across a trailer full of composite letters. I eagerly began pulling them out to see if I could come up with a word appropriate for an entryway coat hanger. I think STUFF says it all!

EXPRESS YOURSELF

Having fun is what the art of inventing with junk is all about. There are no borders when working with castoffs, creating endless opportunities for innovative self-expression. Allow yourself to set your inner kid free to be purely playful—projects born of a sense of humor will be your favorites for years to come. This coat hanger has become one of my favorite happy-go-lucky projects of all time.

BELOW The big and bold letters are affixed to a piece of reclaimed lumber large enough to provide stability without upstaging them. I added in a super-cool metal table to help corral pocket and purse droppings.

BELOW LEFT Vintage hooks are readily available and inexpensive. They add a touch of authenticity to the reclaimed coat hanger.

I have been a collector of letters for as long as I can remember, so you can picture what my reaction was when I discovered a trailer full at a cost between $2 and $5 each. I was giddy as a schoolgirl before her first high school dance! In hindsight, I should have bought all the composite letters, but I'm still delighted with what I did acquire. The task of building the coat rack was straightforward, quick, and easy.

Bear in mind that projects don't have to be difficult or take hours of your valuable time to be terrific. Sometimes the pure joy of discovering the unanticipated while on a shopping excursion and a few hours of deliberation on possibilities will save you time on the actual labor. Playful and painless is the best of both worlds.

TOP RIGHT What can I say? Most people who love vintage are all in. Retro key holders are the bomb!

RIGHT A vintage Stetson and leather jacket ride side by side on the stuff coat rack. The jacket pockets are another storage opportunity.

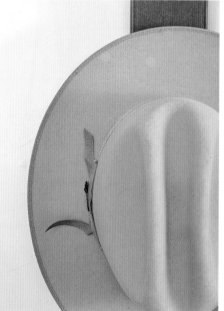

Building with composite wood, especially old pieces, can be tricky because it is not as sturdy as real wood. For best results, purchase only pieces that have been protected from damp conditions.

Old boxes and drawers are another basic in a junker's realm. This numbered goodie is just right for sunglasses and loose change.

STUFF COAT HANGER

We all have stuff, right? Like many of you, I have too much of it, making organization a nightmare. Salvaging these letters put a serious smile on my face. This whimsical project will make getting your ducks in a row entertaining. You might even get kids to hang things up. Stranger things have happened!

MATERIALS NEEDED

- Wood and Metal Finisher's Toolbox (see p. 22)
- Rescued composite letters
- Old 1-in.-thick by 8-in.-wide wooden board, approximately 6 ft. long
- 3 colors of gel stain; I used mahogany, antique maple, and hickory
- 5 vintage coat hooks

TOOLS NEEDED

- Junker's Toolbox (see p. 12)
- Safety First Kit (see p. 18)

SAFETY FIRST

Be sure to wear gloves throughout this project, particularly when working with bleach, stain, and Minwax Polycrylic, as well as old wood.

METHOD

1. Clean the composite letters with bleach diluted with water, then use a shop rag to wash the letters with warm water. Let dry in the sun.

2. Sand the letters with fine- to medium-grit sandpaper. This is easiest with a power sander, but you also can do it by hand with sandpaper or a sanding block.

3. Secure the board to a table with clamps. Measure the wall where your sign will hang, and measure and cut the board to length using a carpenter square and jigsaw. **A**

4. Using a shop rag and warm water, clean the board and allow it to dry, then sand using fine- to medium-grit paper. **B** You only need to sand one side and the edges. Apply 1 coat of Minwax Polycrylic to the sanded side and edges of the board with a shop rag.

5. Measure and mark the back of the board for ½-in. wood screws to use for hanging the coat hanger. Predrill holes where marked, then screw in wood screws, leaving space to attach hanging wire. Measure and cut the wire; then wrap it around the screws. Tighten the screws to secure the wire.

6. Stain all sides of the letters with gel stain, varying the colors across the word. **C** Let the stain dry, then apply Minwax Polycrylic to all sides of the letters. Use a clean shop rag for the stain and a paintbrush for the Minwax Polycrylic.

7. Measure and mark for letter placement on the board.

8. One at a time, glue the letters to the board; clamp until the glue has dried.

9. Before removing the clamps, screw the letters one at a time to the board from the back. I used several 1½-in. wood screws to secure each letter. **D**

10. Measure, mark, and drill holes on the letters for vintage hooks. Then screw the hooks into the letters and hang the sign. **E**

GIVE IT THE BOOT

BOOT TRAY

The busy lifestyles of families these days have you coming and going at a rapid pace. Inclement weather can put a damper on your desire for clean floors. Round up the whole family's lineup of footwear in this tidy tote.

FRESH FROM THE FARM

Salvaged goods from a farm are first-rate candidates for your basic household storage needs because they were built to last. The functionality of this farm find—a chick transporter—is second only to its beautiful form. Galvanized metal treated with several coats of protective polyurethane makes this boot unit highly durable and tough enough to stand up to daily wear and tear. It gets its boost from another industrial find, this time from the plumbing department at a local hardware store. Hex head bushings are just what the foot doctor ordered to give the boot dryer the lift it needed. Tough construction adhesive holds the legs firmly in place.

I made a quick stop in another aisle at the hardware store and picked up a roll of smooth rubber utility mat to place under the tray. With a quick measure and a couple of

My boot receptacle is 38 in. long and can corral five to six pairs of boots. That's a family's worth! The punched holes on the chick transporter allow for natural drainage of wet footwear.

cuts, you'll have yourself a layer of protection between moisture and your floor. It pleases me to no end when functional pieces are on the cutting edge of design.

TWO FOR THE PRICE OF ONE

My boot bungalow needed a playmate, so I designed a coat hanger on the fly after finishing my dryer. That means it's the bonus round for you. Off-the-cuff creations oftentimes turn out to be your best work. If you identify a need, and you needed it yesterday, let your mind hit the ground running. In this case, an old paint store yardstick I had lying about came in handy. I attached three self-adhesive wall mount hangers and screwed the whole contraption to the wall. The entire endeavor took the sum total of 15 minutes. The boot tray and coat hanger go together like peanut butter and honey. I'm sure they will be lifelong buds!

LEFT Here is a bonus for you. I needed a coat rack, so I put hooks on a yardstick. Done deal!

BELOW Sweep up the leaves in style with a handcrafted broom fashioned from cornhusks. The texture is to die for! Looks like the vintage cowboy boots have found a good home.

KNOW HOW

Farmers many times have piles of stuff waiting to be buried, burned, or thrown away, making them ripe for the picking. A visit to a few local farms might be worth a leisurely Sunday drive!

Be sure to shop the plumbing aisle at any hardware store for cool finds like these hex head bushings. The sky's the limit!

MAKE IT

BOOT TRAY

We all know I have a love affair with galvanized metal. This chick transporter is extra special because of the cool pattern created by the punched holes. Who would have thought that a contraption used to haul baby chicks from point A to point B would become a boot tray? That would be me!

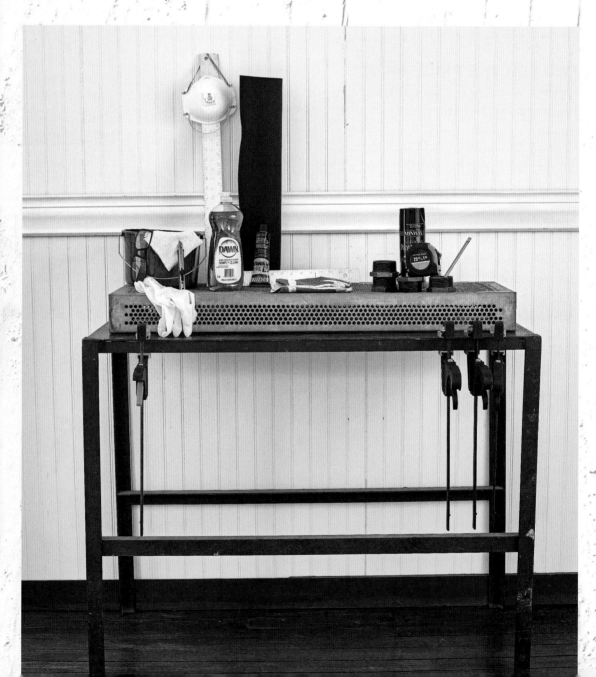

MATERIALS NEEDED

· Wood and Metal Finisher's Toolbox (see p. 22)

· Vintage chick transporter (mine is 14 in. wide by 38 in. long)

· Four 2-in. by 1¼-in. hex head bushings

· 1 roll smooth rubber utility mat, approximately 24 in. wide (make sure the mat is at least 8 in. longer than the chick transporter)

TOOLS NEEDED

· Junker's Toolbox (see p. 12)

· Safety First Kit (see p. 18)

METHOD

1. Clean the chick transporter with a rag and warm, soapy water.

2. Working with 1 bushing at a time, apply construction adhesive to the top of the threaded part. **A** Using the holes of the chick transporter as your guide, place a bushing at each corner on the underside of the tray.

3. Clamp the bushings to the chick transporter, and allow to set for 24 hours. **B**

4. Measure the length of your chick transporter, then measure and mark the utility mat 8 in. longer. Cut the mat using a carpenter square and multipurpose tool. **C**

5. After 24 hours, remove the clamps. Spray the entire unit with several light coats of polyurethane, allowing each coat to dry before adding the next. Then place the boot tray toward the back of the mat.

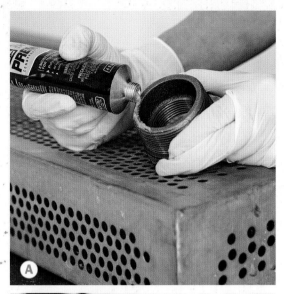

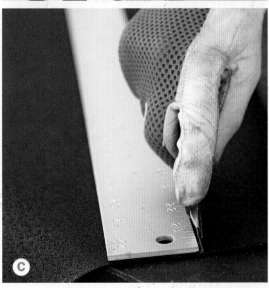

THE KID ZONE!

CHILD'S BENCH

This adorable petite bench is picture perfect for that pint-size princess of yours to remove her outdoor gear before coming inside. I think every child feels special when they have a separate corner of the world to call their very own.

The simplicity of this entryway called for the design of the bench to follow suit. Modern country did the trick.

A CHILD'S BENCHMARK

It's a good idea to teach kids the art of staying organized and keeping their home tidy. Taking boots and coats off before entering the home is a good start, and a bench they can call their own will encourage the behavior by adding a bit of fun to the process. As the little ones grow, the bench can be replaced with a larger model, and this one can be stored away for your children's children. That's one of the reasons I love working with and transforming vintage furniture—with careful thought, you can create family heirlooms

OLD-WORLD CHARM

The finish on the bench is reminiscent of old-world Swedish painted furniture. Milk paint is ideal for this old-world finish because it is old-world paint. Mastering the art of what I call destruction reproduction is easy. You don't have to be particularly neat when painting, as you will remove much of the paint through distressing. After sanding, throw some stain into the mix. I applied a layer of gray penetrating stain, then wiped it away. The gray stain discolored the milk paint, providing an even more aged look. Finishing with a dark paste wax puts the icing on the cake.

This handmade cutie awaits the arrival of your youngster. Dolly is sure to become a treasured family heirloom.

RIGHT AND BELOW The soft white corduroy embellished with old chair webbing works very nicely with the bench's old-world finish.

CHILD'S BENCH

The blue velveteen-like textile on this bench was even more hideous than it looks. It had a lovely rubber backing on it. Ouch! Regardless of how utterly unattractive the bench was, it made me think of my kids and the possibility of grandkids. I hope my children are reading this. Hint, hint!

MATERIALS NEEDED

- Wood and Metal Finisher's Toolbox (see p. 22)
- Crafter's Toolbox (see p. 24)
- Vintage child's bench
- Vintage white corduroy fabric or new fabric of your choosing
- Old or new jute chair webbing
- Approximately 1 yd. of batting
- Milk paint in parchment
- Penetrating stain in gray
- Real Milk Paint Ultra Bond

TOOLS NEEDED

- Junker's Toolbox (see p. 12)
- Safety First Kit (see p. 18)

METHOD

1. Using a screwdriver or multipurpose tool, remove the staples from the back of the bench. Fill the holes with wood filler and smooth with a putty knife. Allow to dry. **A**

2. Remove the upholstered bench seat using a screw gun. Remove the upholstered seat back by tapping it with a hammer. Remove the old fabric and batting from the seat and back.

3. Lay the seat and back on the new batting. Cut the batting, leaving approximately 3 in. extra on all sides.

4. Lay the seat and back on the white corduroy and cut it to a similar size as the batting.

5. Position the seat and back so they are right side up with the batting on top and use an electric staple gun to staple the batting to the seat and back sparingly to hold it in place.

6. Lay out the fabric on top of the batting, right side up. Flip the seat and back upside down and begin stapling the fabric to each. Start at the center point of each side, bringing the extra fabric and batting over the edges of the sides and making sure the fabric is taut. Once this is done, flip the pieces over and check to see if your fabric is straight. If it is, flip the seat and back over again and continue stapling, gently tugging on the fabric to ensure the fabric is taut all around, leaving the corners for last. If the fabric wasn't straight, remove the side staples, reposition the fabric, and check again before stapling all around.

7. At each corner fold the excess fabric to form hospital corners and staple.

8. Measure and cut 2 strips of chair webbing, one to run the length of the seat and the other to run across the width. Be sure you measure for enough to go around the edges of the seat, plus 3 in.

9. Apply fabric adhesive at the edges of the webbing and attach one strip at a time. I attached the widthwise strip first. After the strips are in place, flip the seat over and reinforce the webbing with staples. **B**

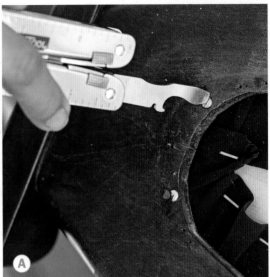

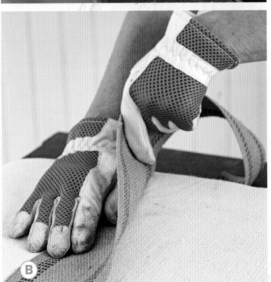

continued on p. 54

continued from p. 53

10. Clean the bench with a rag and warm, soapy water, then sand the bench with fine- to medium-grit sandpaper. Remove sanding residue with a tack cloth.

11. Following the manufacturer's directions, measure and mix the milk paint with water. After the paint is mixed, add bonding agent as directed by the manufacturer. Apply 2 coats of milk paint to the bench, allowing the first coat to dry before applying the second. **C**

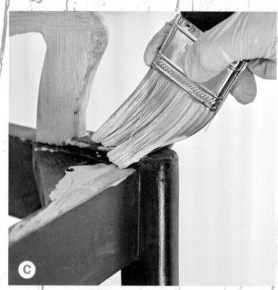

12. Sand the bench with medium-grit sandpaper until you've achieved a heavy distressed look, similar to what you'd see on Swedish painted furniture. **D** Remove residue with a tack cloth.

13. Using a staining pad, apply a light coat of gray penetrating stain to the bench. **E** Wipe it away with a shop rag.

14. Let the stain dry, then apply paste wax to the bench with a shop rag.

15. Reattach the bench seat and back using the original screws and tack nails. If necessary, apply some hot glue to the bench back prior to securing with tack nails.

KITCHEN CAPERS

FUN AND FUNCTIONAL GALLEY GOODS

No matter where I serve my guests, it seems they like my kitchen best. I remember this saying from my childhood and believe it is as true today as it was back then: The kitchen is where families start their days and bring them to a close with that last little nibble before bedtime.

To accommodate your active brood, your kitchen needs to be friendly, functional, and organized. With that in mind, I've dished up some Junk Beautiful galley goodies to help you achieve your kitchen objectives.

WHITE BREAKFAST TABLE

Converting retail merchandising implements is a fabulous way to save viable pieces from the burn pile or landfill. Commercial components are constructed to withstand abuse, making them ideal for a second career in the kitchen. A straightforward paint job paired with a thoughtful embellishment took this industrious table from basic to beautiful.

INSPIRATION POINT

Specimens of an industrial nature are among my favorite furniture pieces to repurpose and revitalize. Fixtures such as retail display units are rough and tumble in character, affording them the ability to withstand whatever is dished up in the kitchen. Being prepared for tough duty does not mean, however, that the finished product should be no-frills, void of warmth and charm. I believe exactly the opposite.

The kitchen this counter calls home provided the inspiration crucial to my vision for revamp. Dark gray cabinets, soft gray walls, crisp white woodwork, and the modern flooring were all taken into consideration when developing my plan. I was also mindful not to completely camouflage the origin of the table. The end result is a softened industrial furnishing that is sweet but not syrupy, making it ideal for its surroundings. Upon completion, the eatery counter was topped with a custom-cut piece of glass and paired with a set of industrial bar stools. Both proffer additional elements with contemporary flair. The set's complete and ready to rumble!

FACING PAGE The pure, fresh, contemporary design of this breakfast counter creation would be stylish and stunning in any home décor.

RIGHT It's totally acceptable and practical at times to mix reproductions, like this juice container, with vintage pieces.

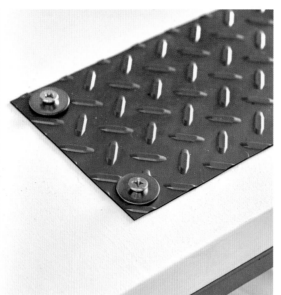

LEFT Who wants their paint to get destroyed? Protect your investment with rubber treads that serve and protect.

BELOW The juxtaposition between the treads and stencil offers an element of surprise!

Fixtures such as retail display units are strong enough to withstand whatever is dished up.

A UNION OF STYLES

My goal for this piece was to soften the hard industrial trade appearance with a modern cottage influence. Bright white paint started the design ball rolling, and the rest fell into place. I chose a soft gray for the border and center stencil to extend the color of its metal legs. The rubberized tread material was a find-of-the-day discovery I stumbled upon at a big box hardware store. The tread is typically used for covering steps, but I fashioned it into foot treads to keep the paint out of harm's way. The treads were glued to avoid puckering, and washers and screws were added at the corners to play up the refined industrial appeal of the kitchen high-top.

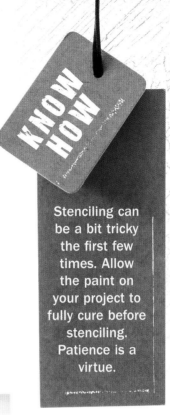

KNOW HOW

Stenciling can be a bit tricky the first few times. Allow the paint on your project to fully cure before stenciling. Patience is a virtue.

LEFT Midcentury glass luncheon sets are ideal for a continental breakfast, for a light lunch, or even for you naughty midnight snackers. Busted!

BELOW Soft and luscious linen napkins are so much better than anything you can find new. Like wine, they get better with age.

4590 B

WHITE BREAKFAST TABLE

A once-humble store display counter gets a face-lift with a fresh coat of paint and some beautiful embellishments. Breakfast at Tiffany's would be nice for sure, but I would be just as happy enjoying a leisurely breakfast with friends or family at this inviting breakfast bar. Time to eat!

MATERIALS NEEDED

- Painter's Toolbox (see p. 14)
- Wood and Metal Finisher's Toolbox (see p. 22)
- Crafter's Toolbox (see p. 24)
- White satin latex paint
- Gray satin latex paint
- Stencil, 10 in. to 12 in. square, in a design of your choice
- Roll of 12-in.-wide rubber mat

TOOLS NEEDED

- Junker's Toolbox (see p. 12)
- Safety First Kit (see p. 18)

METHOD

1. Remove the top and bottom of the display counter. **A** Sand the wood pieces with fine- to medium-grit sandpaper.

2. Remove the sanding residue with a tack cloth. Wash all surfaces with Sunnyside TSP Substitute then wipe them clean with a shop rag and warm, soapy water. Let the surfaces dry.

3. Following the manufacturer's instructions, apply 2 or 3 light coats of stain-blocking primer (I like Zinsser® B-I-N® primer) to the top and bottom of the display table.

4. Using a sponge roller, roll the white paint onto the top and bottom of the table. Apply 2 or 3 coats; let the paint dry completely between coats.

5. Determine how large a border you want to leave around the outside edge of the tabletop. I left a 1-in. border. Measure around the table, and apply painter's tape to the edges. Using a sponge roller, roll on gray paint. **B** You'll probably need 2 coats.

6. Find the center of the tabletop. Place the center of the stencil in the center of the top; use a carpenter square to check that the spacing is even all the way around. Mark the corners of the stencil, and remove it from the tabletop; then tape off the square in the center of the tabletop, positioning the tape at the marked corners. **C**

7. Using a sponge roller, roll on gray paint and allow it to dry.

8. Place the stencil over the gray square and tape it to the tabletop. With white paint and a craft sponge, paint over the stencil using an up-and-down motion, like you're blotting on the paint. Be sure to cover all exposed areas. **D**

9. Measure the base of the table, and cut 2 pieces of the mat with a box cutter or X-Acto knife to a size that fits your table. I cut two 6-in. by 12-in. pieces. Glue the mat to the base of the table on 2 sides.

10. Drill pilot holes for screws to secure the mat; then screw the mat to the base with wood screws and washers. **E**

CHARGE IT!

FLATWARE BOX–CUM–CHARGING STATION

I accepted a challenge from my book editor. Rising to such an occasion is entertaining and a most excellent way to keep your mind on the cutting edge of creativity. The petition was for a pretty, practical, and plausible unit to charge a family's worth of electronic devices. As I recall, it took me approximately 30 minutes to figure it out. I'm not meaning to sound boastful, but it hit me like a ton of bricks why I had purchased the vintage flatware box the day before. Don't you love when that happens? It makes you look all sassy, but the reality is that sometimes you just get lucky!

LAPTOP, TABLET, AND PHONE, OH MY!

The container has two compartments—a top opening and a drawer—making it extremely adaptable for your needs. The top can accommodate a 13-in. laptop or two iPad® mini-size tablets. The bottom drawer can house smartphones for a family of four or a combo of phones and tablets. Now that's what I call getting the job done right!

Be creative—there are countless opportunities for reinvention.

This hardworking unit houses a 13-in. laptop with just enough room to spare for the charging cord.

FACING PAGE Keep your electronic gadgets undercover. My charging station is incognito nestled among kitchen gadgets and cookbooks.

CONTAIN YOURSELF

Folks used to covet their special flatware or silverware, and they carefully stored the sets in wooden chests tucked out of sight in a kitchen cabinet or dining-room hutch only to be brought out on special occasions. That's not how things are done today. The flatware itself is in drawers, so what to do with all of those boxes? I suggest that there are countless opportunities for reinvention, but a charging corral is surely a worthy choice for our contemporary lifestyles.

The containers can easily be found at antique stores or other vintage shopping venues. After you secure a case of your own, you can apply the methods I used while adjusting the process to make the station fit your requirements. It's that easy!

KNOW HOW

The wood used in the construction of flatware chests is a bit flimsy. Use a block of wood for support when drilling holes in the bottoms.

ABOVE Holes were drilled and bumpers applied to keep phones raised from the surface and ventilated while charging.

RIGHT Everyone has their obsessions. Scales are a point of weakness for me.

Decorative craft paper lines the inside of the drawers to disguise
flaws left behind from the removal of the original inserts.

FLATWARE BOX–CUM–CHARGING STATION

The modern world of technology has created a need for more storage. What to do with all of those gadgets? Phones, tablets, computers, and other such electronic devices need a place to call home, too. I was given a challenge, and here is my solution. A vintage flatware case to the rescue—oh happy day!

MATERIALS NEEDED

- Crafter's Toolbox (see p. 24)
- Painter's Toolbox (see p. 14)
- Vintage flatware case
- Lift Off® adhesive remover
- White acrylic craft paint (I used Martha Stewart Crafts® Wedding Cake color)
- Light brown acrylic craft paint
- 4 sheets of decorative craft paper
- 1 roll of decorative craft tape
- Natural-finish decorative wood cutouts
- Self-adhesive craft letters
- Small self-adhesive bumpers (number will vary based on individual devices)
- 4 square self-adhesive bumpers

TOOLS NEEDED

- Junker's Toolbox (see p. 12)
- Safety First Kit (see p. 18)
- 5/16-in. brad-point drill bit
- Drill guide jig

METHOD

1. Remove the flatware holders from the interior of the box. They might need a little coaxing with the edge of a putty knife. Leave the original textile at the top of the cover to identify its origin. **A**

2. Spray the inside of the case and drawer with Lift Off. Once it has absorbed, scrape the surfaces clean with a putty knife. **B**

3. Sand the case first with a medium-grit sanding block and then with a medium-grit pad to clean up any nibs. **C** Remove the sanding dust and Lift Off residue with a shop rag and warm, soapy water.

4. Wearing gloves and a mask, clean the entire case and drawer with Sunnyside TSP Substitute (follow the manufacturer's instructions); then wash with a shop rag and warm, soapy water.

continued on p. 68

continued from p. 67

5. Measure and mark drill holes in the back of the case. **D** The size of the openings will depend on the device(s) you will be storing. I drilled from the back of the box for the USB and charging cords with a ½-in. spade bit. **E**

6. Apply tape where you're going to drill to prevent the wood from splintering. Clamp a block of wood to the case, and use the drill guide jig and brad-point bit to drill the holes. **F** Drill holes in the bottom of the case's top section, the bottom of the drawer, and the bottom of the case for ventilation.

7. Apply primer in 3 light coats. **G** Let each coat dry before brushing on the next.

8. Roll on the white craft paint. Apply 2 coats, letting the first one dry before applying the second coat. **H**

9. I added a 1½-in. light brown stripe, just off center, on the top. Measure for placement and size, then tape off the area. Apply 2 coats of light brown craft paint, letting the first one dry before brushing on the second. **I**

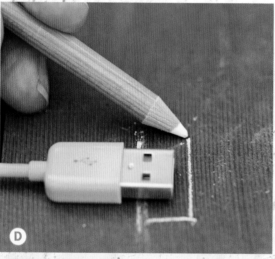

D

E

F

G

10. Using a ruler and black craft marker, outline the edge of the stripe.

11. Measure the top section and drawer bottom and cut craft paper to size. **J** Following the manufacturer's instructions, apply Mod Podge and glue the paper to the case.

12. Measure and cut the craft tape and apply at the edges of the paper. Apply an additional coat of Mod Podge over the paper and tape. **K** Using your craft knife, cut the paper away from the ventilation holes.

13. Adhere the decorative wood cutouts in the position of your choice with super glue. Place self-adhesive craft letters on top of the case, in the position of your choice.

14. Place small self-adhesive bumpers inside the case and drawer to lift the devices for ventilation. Position the square self-adhesive bumpers at each corner of the bottom of the case to lift it and allow for proper ventilation.

COMMUNICATION CENTRAL

CHALKBOARD AND EASEL

Some things never go out of style. A kitchen chalkboard is as suitable today for family communications as it was in days gone by despite smartphone calendar and note-to-self capabilities. I actually find chalkboards a refreshing departure from electronic devices. An aged easel is a wonderful way to showcase the board.

THE DAILY DOUBLE

There are chance moments in life when you get the opportunity to share a big whopper fish tale. This is one of those moments. I was on a mission to find and recover a special something that was prone for repurposing and rendered useful in the kitchen. I immediately spotted the easel, and it gave me pause for thought.

The owner of the establishment, knowing who I was, offered the easel to me for $20, but there was a caveat. Little did I know that the daily steal was about to become the daily double. In order to purchase the easel, I had to take the chalkboard off her hands free of charge. Score! Sometimes, you are in the right place at the right time. The moral of the story is that shopping at a big box outlet will never provide such an exhilarating experience, nor would you be able to purchase items of this quality at a similar price. Now that's what I call a twofer!

FACING PAGE Embracing and revitalizing the natural splendor of the timeworn easel was the ticket to success. Paint was not a requirement.

BELOW LEFT Fancy up your chalkboard with a painted-on stencil. Use a permanent paint pen or washable marker if you want the option for change.

BELOW Bring out your inner child! Colored sidewalk chalk works well and provides for a more playful experience.

RIGHT Mabef has been a symbol of quality for more than 60 years and produces products built to last. Don't cover details like this—it's part of the charm of oldies but goodies!

BELOW RIGHT Spring into action with commonplace coils skillfully on duty as chalk holders.

FACING PAGE After your projects have been completed, they need to find other junkables that will play well together in the sandbox. White vintage pottery is definitely an abiding favorite and can be called upon to manage many utilitarian demands.

BREAKING FAMILY NEWS!

The chalkboard is ginormous, offering plenty of room to write lists, jot notes to your family, or publish a weekly calendar. That's fine and dandy, but I thought it was just a wee too much black to leave it totally buck naked. My long-established approach to design is not to underdo and not to overdo. I liken it to the story of the three bears—what you want upon completion is something just right!

With a chalkboard as my focal point, the stenciling with a chalk pen seemed like an appropriate choice. The pretty design combined with the playfulness of the springs and chalk set the stage for a thoughtful environment. An old stool and white pottery are perfect partners and provide a warm yet current setting.

Chalkboards are a refreshing departure from electronic devices. An aged easel is a wonderful way to showcase the board.

MAKE IT

CHALKBOARD
AND EASEL

Family messaging made easy. A lonely chalkboard unites with its new friend the easel to become a cute and clever memo board for use by the whole family. Leave love notes, reminders, or shopping lists in one convenient place. No one will ever wonder where to look for messages with a chalkboard this prominent!

MATERIALS NEEDED

- Painter's Toolbox (see p. 14)
- Toothbrush
- Howard Feed-N-Wax
- White satin latex paint
- Stencil in a design of your choice (make sure it fits the chalkboard area)
- White chalkboard marker
- Spray clear coat (optional); I like Rust-Oleum Chalked Matte Clear
- 2 coil springs

TOOLS NEEDED

- Junker's Toolbox (see p. 12)
- Safety First Kit (see p. 18)

METHOD

1. Clean the base of the easel with straight vinegar to remove mold. Use a toothbrush to get into tight corners, then wash with a damp rag and warm water. **A**

2. Sand the easel and chalkboard frame with a fine- to medium-grit sanding block or sandpaper. Remove the residue with a tack cloth.

3. Condition the easel with Howard Feed-N-Wax. **B**

4. Tape the chalkboard in preparation for painting the frame.

5. Apply stain-blocking primer to the chalkboard frame. Apply 2 or 3 light coats, letting them dry in between. **C**

6. Paint the frame with 2 or 3 coats of white latex paint; let each coat dry before applying the next. Then apply Minwax Polycrylic to the frame and easel.

7. Position and tape the stencil to the chalkboard. Using a chalkboard marker, fill in the stencil. **D**

8. If desired, tape off the chalkboard around the stencil with cardboard, and spray over the stencil with spray clear coat.

9. Attach the coil spring chalk holders with super glue or epoxy. **E**

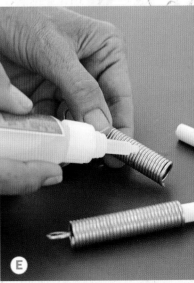

FRESH FROM THE KITCHEN

KITCHEN WINDOW HERB GARDEN

I like to fancy myself a chef. Some may argue with that, but I prefer my own misguided reality. Anyhoo, the kitchen is clearly for cooking, and nothing puts the yummy in a flatbread like fresh-cut herbs. This herb patch sprouts from old glass lampshades. Now that's a bright idea!

FROM SILL TO TABLE

Yes, as junkers, we enjoy the thrill of the hunt, the act of repurposing, and enhancing our homes with vintage gems. I think, however, that junking is farther reaching than that. For me, it's about an all-encompassing lifestyle. Making the conscious choice to refashion furniture and accessories rather than buy new goes hand in hand with living healthy, eating well, and being respectful of our environment. Are you with me? This is why I introduce and use organic materials in many of my projects.

My kitchen windowsill herb garden is a fine example of incorporating these ingredients. The construction was easy, and the materials are readily available. This plot of herbs doesn't care if you live on a farm, in a suburban neighborhood, or in a loft in the city. It is user-friendly wherever you call home. To achieve success in windowsill gardening, select herbs that are hearty and called for often in recipes, and have your tools to care for them close at hand.

My thrift-store lampshades needed partners. Tree cookies harvested from fallen branches found in neighboring woods filled their dance cards.

Lining a plant container with moss will keep the soil moist for a longer period of time. What that means is greater chance for success!

BELOW The lampshade makes an elegant transformation from herb coffer to candleholder. Unleash your imagination and refresh your projects by rethinking their possibilities.

TOP The beauty and bouquet of fresh herbs are enticing properties in a cook's kitchen. Grow some yourself!

ABOVE Keep a gizmo for clipping close at hand. Antiquated scissors—that's the ticket!

KITCHEN WINDOW HERB GARDEN   77

MAKE IT

KITCHEN WINDOW HERB GARDEN

I am a fanatic for fresh, so this little project is right up my alley! The lampshades were found at my local Habitat for Humanity® ReStore®, while the vintage holders were uncovered at a friend's work shed. What would a girl do without cohorts? As for the tree limb, I had a brush with nature.

MATERIALS NEEDED

- Wood and Metal Finisher's Toolbox (see p. 22)
- Crafter's Toolbox (see p. 24)
- Small tree limb (mine is 5 in. in diameter)
- 3 vintage chimney lampshade holders
- 3 thrift store glass lampshades
- Potting soil
- Three 4-in. potted hearty herbs, such as rosemary, thyme, and oregano

TOOLS NEEDED

- Junker's Toolbox (see p. 12)
- Safety First Kit (see p. 18)

METHOD

1. Clamp the tree limb to your worksurface. With gloves on, peel and remove as much bark as possible from the entire limb. **A**

2. Cut 3 tree cookies to your desired thickness using a bow saw. **B** Mine range from 1 in. to 3 in. in thickness to create a pleasing height difference.

3. Sand the bark off the tree cookies using medium-grit sandpaper on a hand sander to create a smooth finish. Also sand the top and bottom of the cookies. **C**

4. Remove all sanding residue with a shop rag and warm, soapy water. Allow to dry.

5. Apply paste wax with a shop rag, then buff.

6. Create a circle groove in the center of each tree cookie with your drill and a 2⅛-in. hole saw. **D**

7. Apply super glue to the lip of the lampshade holders and twist into the hole saw grooves. **E**

8. Place each lampshade inside a lampshade holder. Line each glass lampshade with moss. Plant herbs and top with additional moss and decorative rocks. **F**

EAT, DRINK & BE MERRY

DINING ROOM DIGS

If you're a foodie like me, the dining hall is most likely a go-to locale in your abode. I always come running when called for dinner and relish in good company, good eats, and fine wine. Whether you're single, married without kids, or have a whole brood on board, this is the place where guests and family should be required to check their cell phones at the door. It's amazing what you can learn through conversation over a leisurely dinner. Dining room furnishings and accessories should be comfortable and inviting to encourage peeps to sit down and enjoy.

A TOM SAWYER DINING SET

MODERN DINING TABLE AND CHAIRS

Applying a whitewash finish is one of the quickest ways to rescue a furniture piece in need. This technique, borrowed from the one and only Tom Sawyer, was just made for modern makeovers like this midcentury table and chairs. The striated look it creates is absolutely stunning.

A SUNDRY SET

There are many people in this world who love auctions. I'm not an auction goer, but I can still reap the rewards without spending an entire day at the auction house. The folks who attend live sales inevitably end up with a lot of product that makes its way to storage. One of my favorite outbuildings to pick from is neatly organized and has goat paths for shopping ease. I first found the table legs, then uncovered the top, then discovered the set of four matching chairs, and lastly picked a set of chairs of a different variety that would work well for the heads of the table. An hour in a shed rather than a full 8-hour day at an auction makes me a happy girl. Once I got everything back to my shop, I assessed its overall condition and determined the direction I would take to enrich its modern appeal.

The whitewash finish enhances rather than entirely covers the original contemporary blond wood of this dining table and set of chairs. Once refinished, the mishmashed grouping would have you believe that the table and chairs came as a matched set.

A NATURAL BLOND

The sleek lines of my dining room set and the blond wood established its path to restoration. I did not want to alter its character to a great degree, but the condition of the veneer needed some tender-loving care. Whitewashing seemed to be the most obvious choice. After making the required repairs, I picked up my paintbrush, wiping cloth, and watered-down paint, and went to work. The way the veneer accepted the paint was a very pleasant surprise! A transparent streaked finish was my goal—and that's exactly what I got.

After the wood was refinished, the recovering of seat cushions began. I selected a colorful pattern to complement the set, with buttons to complete the look and add a surprising touch. I opted to keep the accessories to a minimum in keeping with contemporary guidelines.

ABOVE A reclaimed board with some detailing holds vintage metal ball finials, crusty pots, and a wee bit of nature.

RIGHT Go the extra mile when reupholstering furniture. The simple addition of a button embellishment completes the look of my seats.

KNOW HOW

Paint does not fix all evils. Take the time to make necessary repairs to wood veneer prior to applying paint.

ABOVE The triangular inlays on the table legs made way for a detail opportunity. The argyle pattern is in keeping with the minimalist design of the table.

RIGHT My back alley rescue was found wearing a shell bikini and bathing cap. I gave her a more refined appearance.

MODERN DINING TABLE AND CHAIRS

The sleek design of this table is very unique, particularly the legs. It almost has a *Jetsons* quality about it, if you catch my drift. The blond wood was not in good enough condition to leave as it was, but with a little glue and a paint wash, I was able to successfully salvage it.

MATERIALS NEEDED

- Wood and Metal Finisher's Toolbox (see p. 22)
- Painter's Toolbox (see p. 14)
- 1 midcentury modern dining table
- 4 midcentury modern side chairs
- 2 midcentury modern end chairs
- White flat latex paint
- Gray flat latex paint
- Approximately 4 yd. of new fabric
- 1 large package of upholstery foam
- 1 large package of batting
- 6 buttons (1 per seat)
- Embroidery thread
- Large needle

TOOLS NEEDED

- Junker's Toolbox (see p. 12)
- Safety First Kit (see p. 18)

METHOD

1. Remove the cushions from the chairs.

2. Wearing gloves and a mask, clean all wood surfaces with a rag and Sunnyside TSP Substitute. Clean all wood surfaces with a rag and warm, soapy water. Wipe dry.

3. Identify any loose veneer, apply wood glue, and clamp. Allow to dry.

4. Very lightly sand all wood surfaces with fine-grit sandpaper; go gently over any repaired areas, but be sure you sand off any glue so the area is flush with the rest of the surface. Remove all residue with a tack cloth.

5. Measure and mix 1 part white latex paint to 1 part water. **A** If the mixture is too thick, add more water a little at a time. The mixture should be runny with a continuous drip from the stir stick.

6. With a chip brush and working in one small section at a time, apply paint to the wood surfaces (except the fronts of the table legs), then wipe it away with a shop rag. **B** Repeat until all surfaces are covered with whitewash. Let dry.

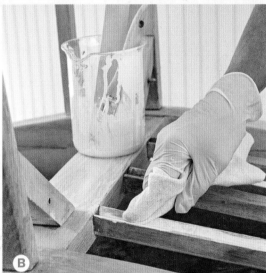

7. Tape off a diamond pattern on the front of both table legs. Paint 2 vertical triangles with 1 coat of whitewash, wipe away, and allow to dry. Remove the tape and reapply to form horizontal triangles. Make a gray wash by measuring and mixing 1 part gray latex paint to 1 part water, until the consistency is the same as with the whitewash. Paint the horizontal triangles with gray wash, wipe away, and allow to dry; remove the tape.

8. Using a carpenter square, define the triangles by marking straight lines with a black paint pen. **C** Let dry.

continued on p. 86

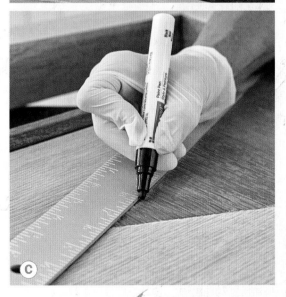

continued from p. 85

9. Apply Minwax Polycrylic to all wood surfaces with a chip brush and let dry.

10. Remove all old fabric and padding from the chair seats.

11. Measure to find the center of each chair seat and drill 2 small holes ¼ in. off center on each side. **D**

12. Measure and cut upholstery foam to fit each chair seat.

13. Measure and cut batting for each chair seat, allowing at least 3 in. of surplus batting on all sides.

14. Measure and cut fabric for each chair seat, allowing at least 3 in. of surplus fabric on all sides.

15. Working with 1 seat at a time, place a piece of foam on top of the chair seat, then top with batting. Flip the seat upside down and use an electric staple gun to staple the batting to the seat sparingly. Tug gently on the batting as you wrap it around the seat and secure it to be sure it's taut.

16. Flip the chair seat right side up and lay a piece of fabric on top of the batting.

17. Flip the chair seat upside down and staple in the center of each side, making sure the fabric is taut. Once this is done, flip the seat over and check to see if the fabric is straight. If not, gently remove the staples, adjust the fabric, and repeat the process. Once the fabric is in the correct position, flip the seat back over and continue stapling around the sides, leaving corners for last. **E** Tug gently on the fabric as you wrap it around the seat and secure it to be sure it's taut.

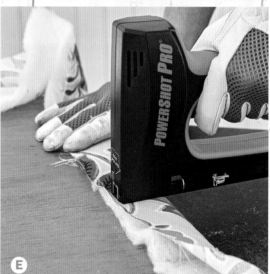

18. At each corner, fold the fabric to form hospital corners and staple. Continue in this method until all chair seats are covered.

19. Thread a needle with embroidery floss and attach a button to the chair seat through the holes drilled previously. Tie off the thread on the fabric side to secure.

20. Reattach the chair seats to the chairs with the screws previously removed at the corners of each chair.

ARCHITECTURALLY SPEAKING

ARCHITECTURAL SALAD SERVER

Architectural salvage is a longtime favorite of mine. You might even call it somewhat of an obsession. These vintage beauties in all of their crumbling glory add a serious dollop of good design to any décor. The main attraction of this dining experience is a reworked base of a classic column.

STEP OUTSIDE THE LINES

I've said it before and I'll say it again: It's all in the mix! From where I sit, the more you step outside the lines, the better your interior design sense becomes. Don't be afraid to shake things up! This modern milieu of black and white was the perfect playground for anything goes. I'll tell you a little secret. When I walked into this location, I knew I wanted to fashion a functional tabletop centerpiece of some sort, but I wanted it to be fresh and innovative, so I employed one of my favorite techniques—the practice of digging through what is at hand and making do with what you find. Spontaneous combustion of a positive nature happens when you do this!

The furnishings commingled with vintage linens, Jadeite dishware, crystal glassware, and contemporary pieces paved the way for my edgy yet ageless architectural salvage salad service piece. By the way, all of the elements for the server were discovered during one rummaging expedition!

ABOVE Floral arrangements don't have to be expensive or time consuming to be drop-dead gorgeous. Simplicity rocks!

FACING PAGE A blend of styles is alive and well in this setting. The combination of industrial and traditional elements is striking.

FACING PAGE A farm-fresh salad is a welcome part of any meal, so why serve it up in a ho-hum manner?

LEFT New old stock drawer pulls fastened with cap nuts provided the finishing touches to the porthole window.

BELOW Retro black-and-white salt and pepper shakers feel at home in this eclectic table setting.

Prior to 1978 all paint contained lead. Be sure to properly encapsulate lead paint with several coats of polyurethane. Reapplication may become necessary with use.

A GORGEOUS GROUP

The inspiration for fashioning my architectural salad server was the grouping of goodies in the room. The sleek metal-top table with salvaged legs thrown together with a tattered bench and modern chairs cried for an architectural embellishment with an industrial twist. Once I got my mojo going, the rest was easy! Two well-worn column base pieces paired with a contemporary porthole window did the trick for me.

The best thing about this project was how effortless it was to create. It's merely an assemblage of objects that can be taken apart with the same ease as they were put together. My vision is a masterpiece salad server, but in the blink of an eye it can be disassembled and dished up in many different and pleasing ways!

SAFETY FIRST
Never put food directly on a vintage piece that could contain lead, even if you've applied polyurethane.

ARCHITECTURAL SALAD SERVER

It doesn't get any easier than this. With basically no tools, a few bits of hardware, and minimal materials, you can compile a sassy salad server in about an hour. The best part is if you tire of it on your table, you can change it up in a matter of moments. Poof you're done!

MATERIALS NEEDED

- Wood and Metal Finisher's Toolbox (see p. 22)
- Crafter's Toolbox (see p. 24)
- 1 two-tiered vintage column base
- 1 bottom of column base
- 1 vintage porthole window

- 3 new old stock hardware
- 3 cap nuts
- 1 round serving bowl, sized to fit on the bottom of the column base
- 1 set of 4 condiment servers, sized to fit on the porthole window around the bottom of the column base

TOOLS NEEDED

- Junker's Toolbox (see p. 12)
- Safety First Kit (see p. 18)

METHOD

1. Wearing a mask and gloves, clean both column bases with a shop rag and warm, soapy water. Clean the metal frame of the porthole window with a shop rag and a solution of 1 part vinegar to 1 part water. Wipe dry.

SAFETY FIRST

Howard Feed-N-Wax is not food safe. Be sure you keep all food in bowls as recommended and on the glass surface of the porthole window.

2. Peel away loose pieces of paint from both column bases. **A**

3. With a wet/dry sanding block, wet-sand the paint on both column bases, removing any remaining loose bits of paint. **B** Allow to dry.

4. Apply Howard Feed-N-Wax to the bare wood on both column bases. **C** Allow to dry, according to the manufacturer's instructions, then buff with a clean rag.

5. With a chip brush, apply several light coats of Minwax Polycrylic to both column bases to seal and encapsulate paint. **D**

6. Apply hot glue to the back of each of the new/old stock pulls and insert into the brackets on the porthole window. Allow to set.

7. Apply hot glue to the inside of each of the cap nuts and attach to the opposite side of each of the 3 brackets on the porthole window. **E** Allow to dry.

8. Assemble the serving tray, beginning with the two-tiered column base, followed by the porthole window, and topped with the column base bottom. Finish the assembly with the serving bowl and condiment servers.

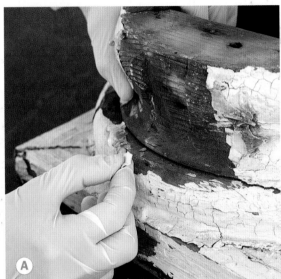

CONVERTIBLE CABINET

INTENTIONAL CRACKLE GLAZE SIDEBOARD

A convertible cabinet is a furnishing staple that's suitable for any dwelling. From use as a sideboard in a formal dining room to a divider in a city loft, this piece goes the distance. Although this project takes longer than a weekend to complete, the end result is well worth your time commitment.

LAYERS OF LOVE

"Take it one layer at a time" is my catchphrase for this cupboard. When I laid eyes on this sizable cabinet, I knew instantly what finish I wanted to use. The piece was prime for painting, as its former owner had reworked its original structure. It was a mishmash of both old and new wood tooled together in a most unusual fashion. It was nevertheless incredibly sturdy and hard wearing. Always keep in mind: Paint is not nails, screws, or glue. A coat or two of any kind of paint can't put Humpty Dumpty back together again. If you pick up an object beyond repair, you're far better off salvaging the parts that remain in good condition and holding on to them for a future project.

With that said, this piece was not in that state, and an intentional crackling process was the solution to conceal its blemishes. The end result is a timeworn finish that's not shiny and new but perfect in its own way.

FACING PAGE Layer upon layer of product, elbow grease, and close attention to instructions will yield a to-die-for furniture finish.

BELOW This white-and-brown pottery is so charming and befitting of this richly restored cabinet. Paired with soft, subdued white pottery, the cluster forms a timeless tabletop.

ON THE FLIP SIDE

You can go from traditional to contemporary in a blink of an eye. Although each side of the cabinet is poles apart in design, the two are fused with the rich gray color. If you have a room that calls for one-sided staging, I recommend repositioning this cabinet with the seasons. The cooler months lend themselves nicely to the solid gray, while spring and summer might be best represented by the eclectic green alternative. If you have an open floor plan, you don't have to flip! You can show off both sides of the coin at the same time, with the open side servicing a different household space. Position the open side toward a gathering space, and utilize the storage for items other than dishware.

FACING PAGE Take a look at the flipside. It's decidedly more modern and colorful.

ABOVE RIGHT Intentional crackling is the technique of applying crackle glaze only where a section would have naturally worn.

BELOW Put pebbles and apples on display in old drawers. It is a refreshing departure from traditional floral arrangements.

KNOW HOW

Practice makes almost perfect. If you are new to a finishing technique, rehearse it on a scrap board similar in nature to your intended piece.

97

4590 B

INTENTIONAL CRACKLE GLAZE SIDEBOARD

A big job, yes! The end result, however, was well worth the time and effort. This finishing technique is called intentional crackling. You only apply the crackle glaze where you believe crackling would have occurred with age. What you end up with is a rich and luscious finish that is both beautiful and believable.

MATERIALS NEEDED

· Wood and Metal Finisher's Toolbox (see p. 22)
· Vintage wooden store counter or other wooden cabinet
· Valspar gray-tinted primer
· Valspar dark gray satin latex paint
· Valspar crackle glaze
· Valspar lighter gray flat latex paint
· Dark brown gel stain

TOOLS NEEDED

· Junker's Toolbox (see p. 12)
· Safety First Kit (see p. 18)

METHOD

1. Using a power sander with fine- to medium-grit sandpaper, sand the large, flat surfaces of the cabinet; then with a fine- to medium-grit sanding block, pad, or paper, sand the details of the cabinet. Remove residue with a tack cloth. **A**

2. Wearing gloves and a mask, clean the cabinet with a shop rag and Sunnyside TSP Substitute. Spray the cleaner on the rag—never directly on the piece. **B** Wash the counter with a rag and warm, soapy water, and let dry.

3. Using a paintbrush or roller, apply tinted primer in 2 or 3 light coats, allowing each coat to dry before applying the next. **C**

4. Using fine-grit sandpaper or a sanding block, lightly sand the primer, which raised the grain of the wood. Wipe off sanding residue with a tack cloth.

continued on p. 100

continued from p. 99

5. On flat surfaces, roll on 1 coat of satin latex paint. **D** Use a paintbrush on details to be sure you get into the nooks and crannies. Allow to dry overnight.

6. Apply crackle glaze to the areas where you want the paint to crackle; use a ¼-in. nap roller. Only roll in one direction. Allow to dry for 1 to 2 hours so that the glaze is tacky, not completely dry. **E**

7. Apply the flat paint over the crackle glaze. Paint in one direction only, making sure the paintbrush is loaded with enough paint to cover in 1 coat. **F**

8. Apply paint to the rest of the cabinet, brushing or rolling depending on the detail on the space. Allow the paint to dry completely.

9. Distress the cabinet with fine-grit sandpaper where desired. I did this around all the edges as well as on the details on the paneled side of the cabinet. You want the distressing to look real.

10. Using a staining pad, apply gel stain to the entire cabinet. **G**

11. Apply polyurethane to all surfaces and let dry.

SKIP TO MY LOO

BREATHTAKING BATHROOM FURNITURE AND STORAGE

When I was growing up, we only had one bathroom. I also had the usual set of parents, one older sister, and four older brothers. I sense you know where I'm going with this. The battle for the little girl's room! My childhood defined how I feel about the bathroom today. It should be a place that's well organized while offering uninterrupted relaxation rather than a constant fight for privacy and alone time. With that in mind, I would like to introduce you to a few bathroom ideas that lend themselves nicely for orderly retreats that are beyond spa-licious.

A CUSTOM CURIO

CRAFTY CURIO CONVERSION

Broken furniture should not always get a one-way ticket to the burn pile. In many cases, a casualty can sometimes be turned into something more sensible for everyday use. Other than door glass unaccounted for, this curio was in excellent condition. Having no operational door to open and close provides much easier access.

CURIO FINDS A HOME

The thought of wallpaper generates a mixed bag of emotions for me. I can never quite decide if I like it or not. This bathroom, however, made me eagerly jump on board the wallpaper bandwagon. The vintage-inspired paper paired with the beadboard wainscoting produced a mouthwatering combination. Upon seeing this bathroom, I knew instantly that my curio cabinet had found a place to call home.

The soft, almost worn-looking colors in the wall covering were the catalyst for my cabinet color choice. I wanted the cabinet to reflect the time-worn look of the paper, so I chose a soft sage gray and lightly distressed it to make it look as though it had been gently used throughout the years. After painting, I thought my piece could handle some additional detailing. The shelves were the next targets on my makeover mission. I refinished the glass to resemble vintage mercury glass. Although this process is often used on glass vases and jars, I thought to myself, why not glass shelves? It's the perfect finish.

FACING PAGE A lightly distressed milk paint finish in a beautiful shade of sage gray presented my cabinet with an entirely new personality.

RIGHT Whoa...wait a minute! There are curiosities outside the cabinet? Of course, some things were made to be handled.

BELOW My curio can hold just about everything you need for the bathroom. From bath towels to everyday toiletries, it's got you covered.

BELOW RIGHT Although the glass is missing in action, the escutcheon was preserved in tribute to the curio cabinet's former operational door.

KNOW HOW

Apply the mercury glass finish to the underside of each shelf rather than to the top. This saves on wear and tear from everyday use.

A MERCURY MISSION

The shelves were super simple to do. There's more than one product on the market to accomplish the task, but I used Krylon Looking Glass spray paint along with a half-and-half vinegar-water solution. You can produce a light veneer or a heavier finish depending on your desired look. The product duo is easy to manipulate. If you don't get what you want the first time around, you can slap on another layer.

I chose a lighter covering because I didn't want the shelves to compete with the paint finish on the curio cabinet. The bonus feature is that the shelves cast a lovely reflection on the mirrored back of the cabinet without my having to go to the effort of applying the finish to the mirror.

ABOVE All-natural hand-poured soaps are ready when you need them neatly tucked into a vintage-linen-lined old box.

LEFT You can't have fresh flowers every day, but a bouquet is a welcoming touch for special occasions and special guests. They are unexpected when tucked inside the cabinet.

CRAFTY CURIO CONVERSION

An elegant bathroom requires refined furnishings. In search of such a piece, curiosity got this cat when I spotted a curio cabinet with a glassless door. I don't enjoy dusting, so I put the cabinet back into play as something more practical for holding bath necessities.

MATERIALS NEEDED
- Painter's Toolbox (see p. 14)
- Old curio cabinet
- Grounding wire (optional)
- Real Milk Paint in Sage Grey

TOOLS NEEDED
- Junker's Toolbox (see p. 12)
- Safety First Kit (see p. 18)

METHOD

1. Remove the glass shelves, then remove the backsplash from the top of the cabinet.

2. Wearing gloves and a mask, clean the wood with Sunnyside TSP Substitute. Wipe down the wood with a clean rag and warm water, then sand the wood with fine-grit sandpaper. You can use a handheld power sander, but be careful not to oversand. **A** Remove any sanding residue with a tack cloth.

3. Tape off the glass with painter's tape.

4. Measure and mix the milk paint, making a solution of 1 part milk paint to 1 part warm water (follow the manufacturer's directions). **B** Shake thoroughly. Once the paint is mixed, follow the manufacturer's directions and mix 1 part Ultra Bond to 3 parts milk paint.

5. Apply the paint to the wood for your desired coverage. **C** I applied 3 light coats. Let each coat dry before adding another.

6. Distress the paint with a fine-grit sanding block, **D** then apply paste wax with a shop rag to all wood surfaces.

7. Clean the glass shelves. Apply Krylon Looking Glass spray paint in small bursts to the bottom of each shelf. Allow to dry (but not completely) following the manufacturer's instructions.

8. Spray the underside of each shelf with a mixture of 1 part water to 1 part vinegar. Dab on the liquid with a shop rag to create a mercury glass finish. **E**

9. Bend and insert the grounding wire into the holes in the top of the curio cabinet from where you removed the backsplash. The wire is optional and purely decorative, but it adds a cool touch.

RAISING THE BAR

RUSTIC TOWEL BAR

This cutie pie is literally made from my scrap pile. When developing 30 projects at one time, I amass quite the array of odds and ends that either were left over from a project or were earmarked for a project but later vetoed. Lesson of the day is don't throw away!

FROM RAGS TO RICHES

In a powder room, space is a valuable commodity. You have many of the same storage needs in a tiny bath as you do in a full, so think strategically when designing for the limited space you have available. This little loo was in need of a towel bar and shelf, so I decided to concoct a unit that filled both needs as not to overwhelm the tight quarters.

What about style? The romantic vintage feel of this room is what directed me to my leftovers. I was after the birch in particular, but while digging, the other components just popped up and said hello. I discovered surplus lumber, unused pipe hangers, and crystal doorknobs. It amazes me how the strangest assortment of elements can seem so wrong for each other individually but be oh-so-right when put together. Burrowing through a scrap pile with an open mind can lead to endless possibilities and the creation of uncommonly good furnishings and home accessories.

An offbeat assortment of scrap materials can be fodder for something fabulous. Try your hand at creating from excess materials. Pretty, practical, and plausible are all present in this towel holder.

KNOW HOW

Keeping birch bark preserved is easy. Simply cover it with several coats of a matte finish polyurethane spray. Allow it to dry completely before handling.

ABOVE LEFT The unification of the ladylike crystal doorknob and the masculine pipe hanger may be unconventional, but it works!

LEFT Make your own diffuser using an old bottle, wicks, and an essential oil recipe to your liking.

BELOW Toilet paper is an essential. Highlight it on a tarnished silver tray and mirror. I dare ya!

RUSTIC TOWEL BAR

C ombining remnants from past projects with bits and bobs from your junk pile is the ultimate test in creativity, not to mention a great way to empty your trash without actually throwing it away. Crafting with scrap successfully will leave you with a true sense of accomplishment and a grin from ear to ear.

MATERIALS NEEDED

- Crafter's Toolbox (see p. 24)
- Birch branch, approximately 10 in. long
- Reclaimed board approximately 14 in. long
- 2 vintage crystal doorknobs
- 2 old pipe hangers
- 2 L-brackets to fit your board
- Two $3/8$-in. wooden dowel pins

TOOLS NEEDED

- Junker's Toolbox (see p. 12)
- Safety First Kit (see p. 18)
- Whittling knife

METHOD

1. Clean the reclaimed board with a shop rag and warm, soapy water.

2. Using a bow saw, cut the birch branch so it is approximately 4 in. shorter than the board.

3. Drill a $3/8$-in. hole in the center of each end of the birch branch. The hole should be approximately $1/2$ in. deep. **A**

4. Using a chip brush, apply several thin coats of Minwax Polycrylic to the entire branch. Allow to dry between coats.

SAFETY FIRST

Be sure you have a good grip on the dowel pin before you start whittling. It's short, so keep your fingers out of the way. Always move the knife away from, never toward, your body.

5. Whittle one end of each dowel pin to fit snugly into the openings on the doorknob hardware. Position your hand against a work surface to help steady the dowel pin. **B**

6. Apply wood glue inside the hole in each end of the birch branch, then insert the non-whittled ends of each dowel pin into the holes. Allow to set.

7. Apply epoxy inside the hole in each doorknob, and attach the doorknobs to the whittled end of each dowel pin. **C** Allow the epoxy to set.

8. Measure and mark for the placement of each pipe hanger on the bottom side of the board. I placed mine approximately 3 in. in from each end of the board. Drill pilot holes at

the marks and attach each pipe hanger with wood screws. **D**

9. Measure and mark for the placement of each L-bracket on the bottom side of the board. I placed mine approximately 1 in. from each end of the board. Drill pilot holes at the marks and attach the L-brackets with wood screws.

10. Apply spray polyurethane to the entire hanging unit. When dry, open the pipe hangers, insert the birch branch, and then fasten the hangers.

11. Hang the towel rack on a wall with wood screws. It is best to secure the towel rack into studs since it will get pulled on as the towel is removed and rehung.

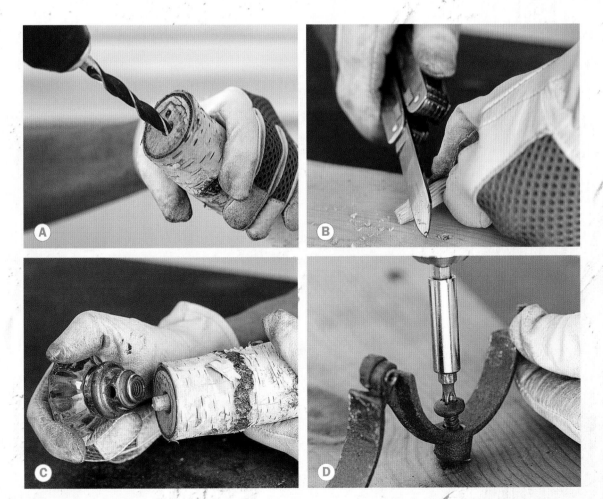

A VISION IN WHITE

LADDERBACK CHAIR BATHROOM CADDY

Chairs have been painted and hung on walls before. I know this. The impetus for my version was to make the chair work hard in a different form than it was intended while maintaining its simplicity in design. This charming chair is both high functioning and drop-dead gorgeous.

Romantic baths are the ultimate sanctuary to soak and soothe weary bones. White—my go-to color for the loo—creates a bath that is crisp, neat, tidy, and inviting.

ACCOMMODATING CADDY

Bathrooms tend to be on the small side and don't typically have a ton of available wall space. Why then litter up your bathroom walls with an army of organizers when just one will do the trick? Bath caddies are at their best when they are devised and assembled to perform a legion of everyday duties. This multitasker came to fruition as well as I had imagined it would. It's a hip-hooray kind of day when that happens.

Chairs of this type are abundant in the marketplace with good reason. Their small seats and rigid straight backs make them incredibly uncomfortable for sitting. I refer to them as in-law chairs. Pull one out when the in-laws come for a visit, and they won't stay long! With a seat that's not suitable for sitting, I chose a new chair chore. This organizer holds towels, bath scrubbies, soaps, loofahs, and more. Don't forget to notice the available rungs on the chair. They could be used to hang your robe, jammies, or a fresh set of clothes for the day. Don't you just love options?

KNOW HOW

When choosing wall hangers, check the packaging for weight recommendations. I purchase ones with more weight capacity than is needed. Better safe than sorry!

BELOW LEFT Gussied-up vintage bottles come into play as shampoo and bath gel containers. They are so much prettier than plastic!

BELOW The vintage pitcher and basin duo is a perfect fit for the chair seat and lodges plenty of bath goodies. Porcelain hooks allow for at-hand storage of larger bathing essentials.

MAKE IT

LADDERBACK CHAIR BATHROOM CADDY

L adderback chairs are a dime a dozen and can be used in a variety of projects. Normally, I would hesitate painting one of these beauties, but the wood was heavily chipped, marred, and stained in some areas, diminishing any true monetary value. Painting and adding hardware put this chair back to work as a bathroom accessory.

MATERIALS NEEDED

- Painter's Toolbox (see p. 14)
- Vintage ladderback chair
- Annie Sloan Chalk Paint® in Pure White
- 3 decorative single 2-in. porcelain hangers with screws included

TOOLS NEEDED

- Junker's Toolbox (see p. 12)
- Safety First Kit (see p. 18)

METHOD

1. Clean the wooden parts of the chair with a rag and warm, soapy water. Let dry, then sand the surface using a medium-grit sanding block or sandpaper. **A** Remove sanding residue with a tack cloth.

2. Apply primer in 3 light coats. **B** Once dry, sand any drips using a fine-grit sanding block or sandpaper.

3. Apply Annie Sloan Chalk Paint, following the manufacturer's directions. I recommend 2 or 3 coats. Allow the paint to dry overnight before proceeding.

4. Distress the paint where desired with a fine-grit sanding block or sandpaper. **C** Clean up sanding residue with a light sweep of a tack cloth.

5. Wearing a protective mask or respirator and working in a well-ventilated area, apply a coat of chalked matte clear protective topcoat. Apply 1 or 2 more light coats a few minutes apart. Let dry. **D**

6. Drill 2 pilot holes on the chair back for D-ring hangers. Choose a bit that matches the inner diameter of the threaded part of the screw, not the diameter of the threads.

7. Position the hangers over the pilot holes and attach to the chair with 1-in. wood screws.

8. Measure and drill pilot holes for each of the porcelain hangers on the front of the top back slat. Position the hangers over the pilot holes, and attach with screws. **E**

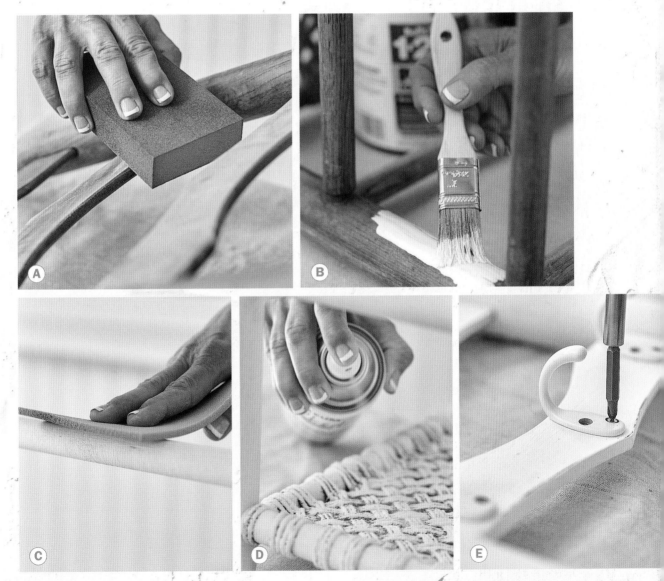

GATHER ROUND

INVITING PIECES FOR INSPIRED GATHERING ROOMS

Rooms that generate a call to congregate are among my favorite household quarters. Family get-togethers, game nights, social gatherings, and other special events deserve furniture and frills that provide a footloose and fancy-free flair to your shindig headquarters. Gathering rooms are great spaces to allow your imagination to run free with party-pleasing projects that put the fun in your family and friends' festivities. A ladder converted to a libation station, a boys' night out game table, and an adjustable side/ coffee table perfect for a movie and popcorn evening in are just a few examples to whet your whistle.

GAME ON!

DEWALT GAME TABLE

Let's chalk one up for the guys (no pun intended!). Through personal experience, I have concluded that men light up like firecrackers at the idea of a getaway just for them. When I spotted this rusty DeWalt® tablesaw base, I knew I had uncovered the start of something rough and tumble.

BOYS JUST WANT TO HAVE FUN!

Cyndi Lauper should not have excluded the gentlemen in her 1980s hit. Boys deserve a good time, too, after all! Upon the discovery of my go-to vintage piece—the DeWalt base—my task was to determine the best way to make it a game table for serious card players. Reclaimed lumber would have been optimal, but many times it is not readily available and often hard on the pocketbook. I decided to take an alternative route and produce a tabletop that was an impressive imposter for the real deal. If I were not to point it out, no one would be the wiser. That's what I call a "gotcha" moment.

A family heirloom pool table rich with recollection needed a partner to enhance this man cave. DeWalt to the rescue!

The tabletop is constructed of six 2-in. by 8-in. by 48-in. boards cut to size by my local hardware store. Why cut it yourself when someone else will do it for you? The rest is in the finish. Paint on a little black tea followed by a coat of steel wool soaked in white vinegar and finish with paste wax.

BOYS AND THEIR TOYS

After the card table was built Ram tough, it was ready to be decked out. I constructed an oversize tabletop so it was ample enough to accommodate the boys and their toys. I admit that I needed to close my eyes and visualize what those toys might include. Hmmm … Doug Smith, my co-conspirator in this project, enlightened me about the "beer and a bump" ritual practiced by menfolk while in their tavern caverns. That was the jumpstart I needed.

Retro pool ball shot glasses, old pilsner tumblers, vintage poker chips, playing cards from the good old days, dice shakers, a bottle opener, and advertising coasters all made the cut. Maker's Mark®, some pilsner, and peanuts were also invited. It wouldn't be a proper partay without them!

Men light up like firecrackers at the idea of a getaway just for them.

TOP RIGHT The rustic finish and masculine detailing of the DeWalt base were flawless for my manitarium mission.

RIGHT This label would get anyone's attention who believes, like me, that tools are way too cool for school.

RIGHT Cool bean accessories make for a very manly beer-and-a-bump moment. Bottoms up!

BOTTOM RIGHT Coasters and a bottle opener are necessary equipment for any man-cave event. I love the graphics on vintage coasters.

BELOW The W. H. Griffith & Co. pool ball rack is a priceless piece at gaming central.

DEWALT GAME TABLE

I t's funny to me how some projects remind me of music from the 1980s. I'll leave you to ponder that. Anyhoo, this is one of the more difficult projects in the book, but well worth the effort. Once you have accomplished a conversion like this, you will feel like you can conquer anything!

MATERIALS NEEDED

- Wood and Metal Finisher's Toolbox (see p. 22)
- Painter's Toolbox (see p. 14)
- Vintage DeWalt tablesaw base
- Six 2-in. by 8-in. by 48-in. boards
- Length of chain

TOOLS NEEDED

- Junker's Toolbox (see p. 12)
- Safety First Kit (see p. 18)

METHOD

1. In a pint jar, make a white vinegar and steel wool solution. Fill the jar three-quarters full with vinegar. Cut half of a pad of 0000 steel wool into small pieces, add to the vinegar, and seal the jar. Let sit for 24 hours.

2. Wipe down the tablesaw base with a shop rag and warm water. Then, in a well-ventilated area and while wearing a respirator or protective dust mask, apply spray polyurethane to the tablesaw base.

3. Prepare the black tea according to the package directions. You'll need about a cup.

4. Distress each of the boards using a chain, screwdriver, and hammer. **A** Tap the chain against the wood with the hammer, leaving marks on the wood. Be sure to apply different pressure on different areas on the wood to create a realistic weathered appearance. Use the screwdriver on the corners and edges of the wood.

5. Apply black tea to the boards with an art paintbrush. Paint one side of the boards at a time. Don't forget to paint the edges, too. **B**

6. Apply the vinegar and steel wool solution to the sides and edges of the boards with an art paintbrush. The tea does not have to be completely dry before applying the vinegar solution. Apply the solution to one side of the boards at a time. Repeat the tea staining and application of vinegar and water solution on all sides of the boards once the first coat is dry.

7. Once the boards are dry, arrange them side by side on the floor, and then turn the tablesaw base upside down on top of them. Center the base on the boards and mark where the top will be attached. Mark each board with a letter or number so you can assemble them in the proper order.

8. Measure and mark the 2 outside sets of boards for 4 or more dowel pins (I used 8). Be sure the marks on each board line up with each other. Using a dowel jig, drill holes for dowel pins in both sets of boards. **C**

continued on p. 122

continued from p. 121

9. Apply wood glue to 2 dowel pins, then insert them into the holes in 1 board. Add additional glue to the edge of the board, attach it to its mating board, clamp, and allow the glue to set. Repeat this process on the other set of boards.

10. Measure and mark the 2 center boards and 2 outside boards for bolts to secure the boards to the table frame. I used four ⅜-in. by 2½-in. hex bolts and nuts. Drill the boards where marked with a ¾-in. spade bit so you can sink the bolts. Wrap the spade bit with tape so you do not drill too deeply. **D**

11. Attach both center boards with nuts and bolts to the tablesaw base. Tighten the nuts with a socket wrench. **E**

12. Attach the outside pairs of boards to the center boards with wood screws where marked. Attach them to the base with nuts and bolts.

13. Finish the wood tabletop with a coat of paste wax and buff.

If you ever feel like you are out of your design element, don't be afraid to use your phone-a-friend freebie chip.

FACING PAGE Let the games begin! The rugged game table is loaded with all the old-school essentials a man could ever want.

GALVANIZED GLORY!

MODERN COFFEE TABLE

I owned the framework for this side table for quite some time. I love the finish of the metal and the frame's clean lines, but I do confess it took me a long while to devise a plan for purpose. It just goes to show you that good things come with time.

MIND OVER MATTER

As I mentioned, it took me some time to figure out what to do with this amazing piece of metal. Sometimes you discover a piece and boom—you know exactly what to do with it. Other times it's not that easy. If you find yourself in this conundrum, don't stuff your prized possession in the garage thinking you will get to it later, because typically you won't. Stuffed away, it will become buried treasure awaiting your next garage sale.

Instead, keep the piece in plain sight. If you pass by it on a regular basis, sooner or later you will have that cherished "aha" moment. I know you know what I mean! It took writing this book to get me to that happy place. In the end, it was quite simple. I cleaned up the metal, being careful not to destroy the patina, and cut wood to insert inside the metal framework. I finished the inserts with a light stain to complement the modern vibe of the frame.

FACING PAGE In keeping with the streamlined metal frame, I elected to complete the table with natural wood inserts.

LEFT Timepieces and weights are just a couple of examples of vintage smalls ideal for displays.

LEFT The patina on the metal of the frame leads me to believe it was formerly an industrial refrigeration implement.

BOTTOM LEFT I deliberately emphasized the corrosion on the metal frame by choosing understated wood panels as the tabletop.

FACING PAGE It's a two-for-the-price-of-one table. The adjustable side of the table goes up and down with ease. When it's time for popcorn and a movie, flip the lid up on this baby. When you're done, just tuck it away! Clocks and gauges are spot-on accessories for a contemporary setting.

TRANSFORMING TABLE

Don't you just love it when something you craft can pull double duty? I sure do! The frame has a side that can be placed in the upward position when needed or lowered when not in use. This ability to transform makes the table far more user-friendly.

When determining how to dress tables such as this, keep in mind you want the movable portion free of clutter so you have available space when you need it. I chose tabletop décor suitable for the style of the table. Modern industrial pieces like clocks and gauges never go out of favor and are common finds in the marketplace. To finish accessorizing, I blended store-bought items with the vintage treasures. There's no rule that everything has to be vintage.

MODERN COFFEE TABLE

An industrious galvanized adjustable frame from origins unknown comes springing back into action as a contemporary coffee table. The patina indicates it may have been used in an industrial refrigeration unit, but that's only speculation. Does it really matter where it came from? Nope! It's cool, and that's all I really care about.

MATERIALS NEEDED
· Wood and Metal Finisher's Toolbox (see p. 22)
· Vintage galvanized adjustable frame
· Various pieces of reclaimed ½-in.-thick wood
· Gel stain in a light color

TOOLS NEEDED
· Junker's Toolbox (see p. 12)
· Safety First Kit (see p. 18)

METHOD
1. Clean the galvanized adjustable frame with a rag and warm, soapy water.

2. Using steel wool and a vinegar solution of 1 part vinegar to 1 part water, further clean the galvanized frame. **A**

3. Using a shop rag, apply paste wax to the galvanized frame, then buff the metal to a nice shine. **B**

4. Measure the inside sections of the frame. Measure and mark wood pieces to fit in the 4 open sections of the frame. If the frame is too wide for your wood, you might need to butt-join 2 pieces to fit; see step 5. Use a jigsaw with a carpenter square as your guide to cut the wood to size. **C** Be sure to cut all pieces of wood to fit snugly within the frame.

5. Two larger sections of the frame required 2 pieces of wood to be butt-joined to fit the openings. Once the wood has been cut to size, apply wood glue, join the pieces of wood, clamp, and allow to dry.

6. Flip the frame upside down and mark the wood for notches to accommodate the frame. Using a coping saw, cut out the necessary notches. **D** Dry-fit the wood to be sure you've cut all necessary notches.

7. Using a staining pad, stain all wood surfaces with a light-color gel stain.

8. Apply epoxy to the inside of the metal frame, insert the wood sections, clamp, and allow to set. **E**

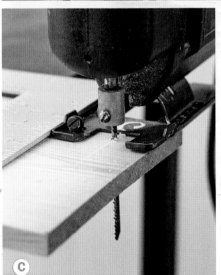

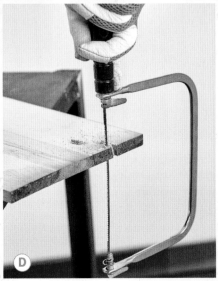

SALVAGE SALOON

LADDER BAR

Old hand-hewn ladders are common fare in the land of junk and regularly employed in projects for the home. What makes this ladder stand out is the quirky combination of salvaged materials used to construct a whimsical workable beverage bar that will put smiles on the faces of your cocktail crowd.

HUMOR ME

Those who know me identify me as a light-hearted being who appreciates a little humor. I never take myself too seriously. Life is short, and I believe we shouldn't go around avoiding obvious pleasures. Having fun is one of those happy places, so go ahead and unleash your playful side in your home décor. The salvage saloon epitomizes this sentiment. In my own home, I include a touch of the funny side in every room. Not belly-wrenching funny, but rather something that gives me a great big Brownie smile each and every time I enter. I actually include humor in the top 10 basics for good design.

FACING PAGE The ladder tavern delivers a full-service refreshment station. No need to leave the room. It's all at your fingertips.

ABOVE RIGHT A certain someone supplied me with a shoebox filled with old drapery hooks. They came in handy for barware hooks.

The liquor ladder exposes its funny bone not only through the crafty collection of junk used in construction, but also through the whimsical assortment of vintage barware. I have to divulge that the carhop caddy was the main catalyst for my task, followed by the silly drink thermometers. These two pilots made for an easy project flight plan.

Old ladders are often worn. Be sure to purchase one that is sturdy, or shore up one that is rickety before attaching your TinkerToys.

RIGHT Plastic swizzle sticks will provide smiles at your social shindig. The cow head certainly made me chuckle!

BOTTOM RIGHT Some things never fall from favor. Glass canning jars are an example.

TIME FOR TINKERTOYS

Project endeavors of a junking nature many times don't involve a mountain of physical effort or an expert level of building know-how. Oodles of ideas occupy more of your time in thought process than in actual construction. You can only imagine how much fun I had at the playground in my mind with this spirits dispenser. Pulling bits and pieces together like canning jars, typewriter rolls, and drapery hooks made me feel like a free-to-be-me little nipper again. I refer to this activity as TinkerToy® time for adults and indulge in it often.

Don't limit yourself to what I have shown, but rather use it as inspiration. Set aside a little playtime of your own and see what the kid in you creates.

TOP LEFT Can you believe this is a working piece from an old typewriter? Just look at its handsome details.

LEFT A&W®, root beer floats, and a carhop in roller skates. Vintage goods are sure to invoke pleasant memories. Enjoy the moment!

BELOW Did partygoers really use such things as drink thermometers? Too darn funny!

LADDER BAR

Here's a fun one for you! Ladders can be found on just about any junk corner, so pick one up and try this project yourself. If you can't find some of the odd fellows I've used for hanging devices, put on your creative thinking cap and see what unusual combination you can carefully concoct.

KNOW HOW

Use a drill bit to get the hole started in each hose clamp before screwing it to the ladder. You can also predrill the hole in the ladder for the clamp. Just line up the holes and attach the clamp with a wood screw.

MATERIALS NEEDED

· Wood and Metal Finisher's Toolbox (see p. 22)
· Old wood ladder
· 3 hose clamps
· 3 canning jars (8 oz., 12 oz., or 16 oz.; I used pint jars)
· Vintage typewriter roll
· 2 broom clips
· 5 old drapery hooks
· Vintage carhop tray

TOOLS NEEDED

· Junker's Toolbox (see p. 12)
· Safety First Kit (see p. 18)

METHOD

1. Clean the ladder with a rag and warm, soapy water, then apply clear spray polyurethane to the ladder. Be sure to work in a well-ventilated area.

2. Measure, mark, and drill a hole in the back of each hose clamp for mounting to the ladder rung.

3. Measure and mark the top rung of the ladder for the hose clamps, spacing them evenly on the rung, then drill pilot holes in the ladder for the clamps. Attach the clamps to the ladder with wood screws.

4. Slip each canning jar inside a hose clamp and tighten the clamps with a screwdriver. **A**

5. Measure the length of the typewriter roll, then measure and mark the ladder for broom clips to hold the roll. Drill pilot holes for the clips; then attach them where marked with wood screws and insert the typewriter roll. **B**

6. Measure and mark the second rung from the top for the drapery hooks, spacing them evenly on the rung. Drill pilot holes for the hooks, then attach them with wood screws. **C, D**

7. Clean the carhop tray with a vinegar solution of 1 part vinegar to 1 part warm water. Mount it on a rung of the ladder as you would on the window of a car. No screws are needed.

THE LIVING IS EASY

CASUAL AND COMFORTABLE FURNISHINGS

As a child, I rarely visited the living room. I often wondered why we would have a room that was used only on special occasions. It didn't make sense to me then, and it doesn't now. When I became a mom, I made the conscious decision to design a living room that was elegant yet casual and comfortable enough for everyday family use. The projects in store for you are a reflection of my informal approach to sophistication. Remember, the junk you've chosen to refresh has the opportunity to become a user-friendly work of art.

RUSTY AND CRUSTY GOODNESS

MEDICAL STAND BLANKET HOLDER

This blanket holder is crafted from a very special find. Sometimes abuse and neglect of a piece can actually leave behind exquisite scars. I don't champion the mistreatment of vintage items, but when I uncover a piece such as this, I do everything I can to turn its warts into pure brilliance.

PASSION FOR PATINA

Are you passionate about stuff in the rough? Me too. I literally spotted this on a pile of junk outside a Quonset hut. I'm not sure how long it had been left to fend for itself in the elements, but from the looks of it, quite some time. I'm also not sure exactly what it was in its glory days. I'm speculating it is a stand from a medical or dental instrument tray, but I could be wrong. It's happened before.

There are times when you needn't be concerned whether you know what something is. In this case, the coolness factor is far more important than the position it filled in its former life. All my mystery reject needed was some tender loving care. My main objective was to enrich, enhance, and encapsulate its already incredible patina. Mission accomplished!

Keep a cozy blanket on a once-abandoned objet d'art next to your favorite chair. This is true junk love.

137

ABOVE LEFT An up-close and personal look at stunning patina exposed after years of neglect and disregard.

ABOVE MIDDLE It's uncanny how seamlessly a hitch trailer ball, also found in the scrap pile, fit the stand's rod.

ABOVE RIGHT Some things take your breath away. The exquisite handle that no longer works remains intact for its sheer beauty.

PRESERVE AND PROTECT

My intent to preserve this piece has already been stated. Upon close inspection, I realized that total restoration was out of the question, so I had to accept my crusty gem for what it had to offer. Due to corrosion, the stand could not be raised or lowered, meaning its height was not open to change. The paint, on the other hand, could be bettered. I measured and discovered the dimensions were right on the money for a blanket holder. Lucky me! A good cleaning, an intentional sanding, and a spray finish did the trick. A bit of whimsy was added by finishing the rod with an old hitch ball that holds the blanket in place.

ABOVE Chamois cloths fashioned into flowers add a sense of softness to this setting. Details make all the difference!

FACING PAGE Damaged and neglected pieces can be brought back into action any way you choose.

KNOW HOW

A lead paint issue can be remedied. Safely wet-sand off the large flakes of paint and encapsulate what remains with several coats of polyurethane.

MEDICAL STAND BLANKET HOLDER

Shut the front door! This thing is over-the-top amazing! I am thinking that this beautifully battered piece is a vintage medical or dental instrument stand with a missing-in-action tray. The absence of the tray allowed me to give it new purpose. It is the picture-perfect piece to hold a blanket.

MATERIALS NEEDED

- Wood and Metal Finisher's Toolbox (see p. 22)
- Vintage medical or dental instrument stand
- Old hitch trailer ball

TOOLS NEEDED

- Junker's Toolbox (see p. 12)
- Safety First Kit (see p. 18)

SAFETY FIRST

When using harsh chemicals it is best to work outdoors whenever possible.

METHOD

1. Wash the metal medical stand with a rag and warm, soapy water.

2. Wearing a mask and gloves, loosen and remove the paint and rust on the stand with an abrasive block. **A**

3. Wet-sand the stand and hitch ball with a medium-grit wet/dry sanding block or sandpaper. **B**

4. Following the manufacturer's instructions, attach the hitch ball to the rod with epoxy. **C**

5. In a well-cross-ventilated space, apply Penetrol to the stand and hitch ball. Be sure you're wearing a mask. **D** Once dry, spray on several coats of polyurethane, letting each dry in between. The polyurethane will encapsulate the lead paint on the stand.

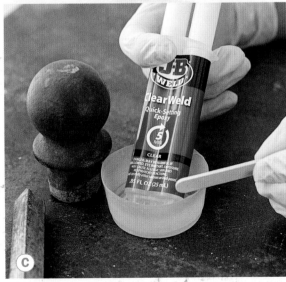

A POTATO PARTITION

ROOM DIVIDER

Industrial black steel pipe and fittings have been used in oodles of DIY projects, so I gave myself an assignment: Design something completely different than I had ever seen before using these materials. One of the things that differentiates this pipe project from others is the use of vintage materials that you just don't come across every day. I am referring to the potato sorter conveyor belts. They are remarkable. I've been a longtime supporter of originality. I hope I passed the test!

A WELCOME GREETING

Greeting your guests in style as they walk through your front door is key. You know what they say about first impressions? My room divider teamed with a vintage chair and the table vignette makes a bold design statement that is very welcoming. The vignette on the table is meant to get a conversation started. It is both whimsical and thoughtful, which can be a tricky combination to achieve, but you can do it!

The combo of flat-out industrial and decidedly shabby is another daring design alternative. I was not certain while assembling all of these various elements that I would be pleased with the outcome, but at the end of the day, I was delighted. I believe risk taking is a basic ingredient in decorating.

FACING PAGE What's the secret sauce? Two fresh-from-the-factory potato sorter conveyor belts hung from a steel pipe frame. This extraordinary divider defines the living room from the entryway while serving as a piece of fine art.

LEFT An old bell with a vintage architectural spindle dresses up the column nicely!

RIGHT Vintage paper is amazing. This old travel journal written in cursive has some fascinating entries.

BOTTOM RIGHT Flanges and hooks are my buddies. They both come in handy for connecting one thing to another.

BELOW A simple glass vessel takes on a new look with a little bit of embellishment à la junk.

The combo of industrial and shabby is a daring design alternative.

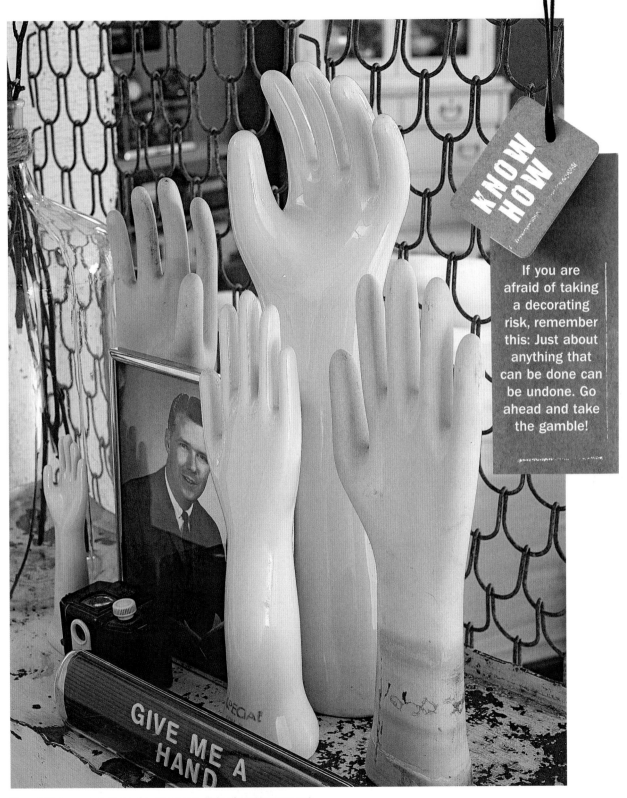

GIVE ME A HAND

Thoughtful presentations are the best. This vignette was put together in loving memory of my good friend's father. Some of the hands are vintage and some are not. Can you tell the difference?

ROOM DIVIDER

P otato sorter conveyor belts are pretty rare, but I have come across a number of them in my journeys. They are stunning hung on your wall as art or done up as a window covering. In other words, they're versatile. If you can't find one, other more typical conveyor belts can be adapted to this project.

MATERIALS NEEDED

· Wood and Metal Finisher's Toolbox (see p. 22)

· 2 sections (approx. 2 ft. wide by 5½ ft. long) of vintage potato sorter conveyor belt

· Two 36-in. by ¾-in. double-threaded black steel pipes

· One 48-in. by ¾-in. double-threaded black steel pipe

· Two ¾-in. black iron floor flanges

· One ¾-in. black iron elbow

· One ¾-in. black iron coupler

· Four 5/16-in. by 5-in. hook bolts (vintage or new)

TOOLS NEEDED

· Junker's Toolbox (see p. 12)

· Safety First Kit (see p. 18)

METHOD

1. Measure and mark the 48-in. pipe for the 4 hook bolts, spacing them evenly. Using a metal punch and hammer, punch the 48-in. pipe where marked. You are making an indentation, not a hole all the way through the pipe. **A**

2. Apply dark thread-cutting oil where marked, then drill a hole through the pipe. Repeat this process until you have drilled 4 holes. **B**

3. Insert the hook bolts into each of the 4 holes in the cross bar and tighten with nuts.

4. Connect 1 floor flange to one end of one 36-in. pipe. Connect the second 36-in. pipe to the first 36-in. pipe with a coupler.

5. Connect the elbow to the end of the 36-in. pipe without the floor flange. **C** Connect the 48-in. pipe to the other end of the elbow, creating the cross bar. Connect the second floor flange to the opposite end of the 48-in. pipe.

6. Working in a well-ventilated area and wearing a mask, spray the black steel pipe frame with 1 coat of polyurethane.

7. Attach the top floor flange to a column, wall, or other steady surface with wood screws. The frame is heavy, so if attaching it to a wall, be sure to screw into a stud.

8. Attach the bottom floor flange to the floor with wood screws.

9. Hang each potato sorter conveyor belt section from 2 hook bolts. Gently knit the sections together where they overlap.

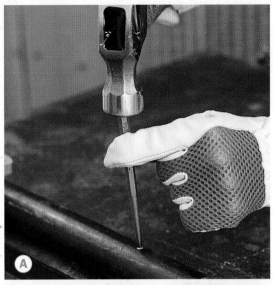

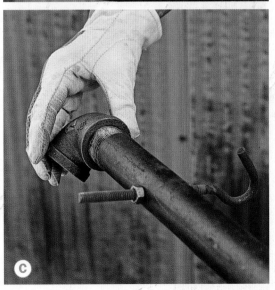

CLEVER SIDE TABLE HACK

WICKER BASKET TABLE

This just may be my favorite project in the book. It's easy, sensible, and attainable, but best of all it's a hack. What is a hack? Simply put, it's taking a piece of furniture and turning it into something completely different and fabulous. This basket was good-looking but not all that practical. It begged for a hack job!

AN UPSIDE-DOWN WORLD

Loved, loved, loved this basket when I found it at a thrift store. It was one of those "had to have it" moments. Not for its intended purpose, mind you, but for its potential. I've said this before: If something is being discarded or sold secondhand and has promise for purpose, go for it! Doesn't matter if it's 10 minutes old or 100 years old.

Giddy with excitement, I whisked the wicker basket home and started to play with it immediately. A good rule of thumb when pondering what to do with your treasure is to look at it from all different angles. Go ahead—flip it upside down, sideways, or inside out if you can! More often than not, this trick will provide you with that gratifying moment. My upside-down basket offered a sturdy base for a table, and that's how the hack was born.

BELOW Here's a tip. Look for vintage accessories in silver and gray. The colors complement the brown wicker.

BELOW RIGHT Vintage shoe forms are a great find—and cool conversation pieces! What say you about resin versus wooden ones? I'll take the resin, please. Awesome sauce!

Don't be afraid to raid your home for components needed to complete your project. I had an extra tree-cookie cutting board that came in quite handy!

RIGHT Natural materials are a welcome touch in any décor. Wicker not only adds beauty, but depth and texture as well. This basket table's upside came from turning its components wrong side up.

BELOW You know me; I'm a pushover for natural materials. The polished rocks add more texture and color.

WICKER BASKET TABLE

This find went from essentially useless to totally functional in the blink of an eye. In less than an hour, a basket can become a terrific table for use in a multitude of home locations. I love it when you can change something dramatically by doing little more than simply turning it upside down. Ta da!

MATERIALS NEEDED

- Crafter's Toolbox (see p. 24)
- Wicker basket, preferably with a top and between 22 in. and 24 in. tall
- Tree-cookie cutting board between 13 in. and 15 in. in diameter
- 20-in. round glass tabletop
- 4 self-adhesive bumpers

TOOLS NEEDED

- Junker's Toolbox (see p. 12)
- Safety First Kit (see p. 18)

METHOD

1. Flip the basket upside down. Find the center of the original basket base and tree-cookie cutting board. With a chalk pencil, make a cross at the center of each using a Speed Square and a carpenter square. **A**

2. Center the cutting board on the basket, and glue it in place. Be sure to apply glue all over the surface of the basket. Place a couple of concrete blocks on top of the cutting board until the glue dries. **B**

3. Turn the basket top upside down. Using your Speed Square and carpenter square, find the center of the basket top and the center of the cutting board.

4. Measure, mark, and drill pilot holes to attach the basket top to the cutting board. Then attach the pieces with wood screws and washers. **C**

5. Fill the basket top with decorative rocks. **D**

6. Attach the bumpers to the outside edge of the basket top and set the glass tabletop in place. Press to secure the glass to the basket.

BED CHAMBERS
SLEEPING QUARTERS DÉCOR

Your bedroom is the number-one go-to spot when you need some serious shut-eye. It's also the place to unwind before you fall into that oh-so-welcome REM sleep cycle. To accomplish comfort and cozy, choose colors, furnishings, and accessory pieces thoughtfully. Don't worry about being on trend—your sleeping chamber is all about you. After all, why would you want to be like everyone else when you can hold the pickles, hold the lettuce, and have it your own way? Sounds reasonable to me. Come along with me and explore some trendsetting bedroom alternatives.

AUSTERE BED RESCUE

BOHEMIAN BED

Being a trendsetter rather than a follower can present challenges—and opportunities. For example, what if you're not in love with the current color trend (mauve? coral? so not my taste!), but that's all you can find in bedding at your traditional retailer? Vintage markets, antique stores, and thrift shops can open your eyes to a whole new style. Blaze new trails, friends!

EVERY PICTURE TELLS A STORY

The story here begins with a simple iron bed found at one of my favorite junk haunts. Rumor has it that it was salvaged from a small-town motel leveled by fire, which explains the soot. I'm fond of the straightforward design of the austere Depression-era bed. After I refurbished the bed, it was time to hop on the rest of the room. My initial thought was cottage, but while junking, everything shifted gears.

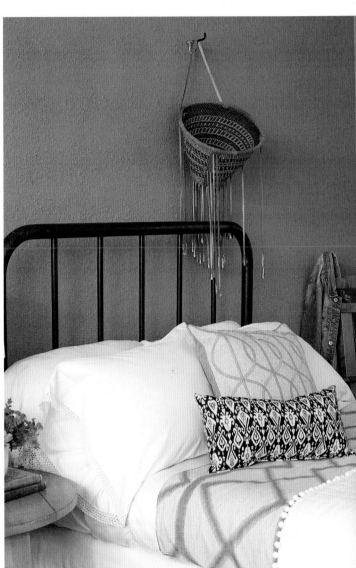

LEFT AND ABOVE The art of the mix is alive and well on this bed. New, old, and repurposed bedding components combine forces. I used a drapery panel to add pattern and color to the bed covering mix.

153

The bedding is lush and layered with an intentional combination of old and new.

After securing the austere bed, my second find was a Kantha quilt. Humble women in Bangladesh originally made Kanthas from vintage sari material. They were handcrafted with love for family members and are fluid and spontaneous in design—just like I encourage you to be. Today, the Kantha is a fair-trade product hand-stitched by Bangladeshi women recovering from abuse. My next discovery was an antique Cherokee burden basket. These were also thoughtfully hand-crafted. No basket was ever made larger than the burden a Cherokee woman could carry. The stories behind these three finds make this room a very special place.

FACING PAGE What was originally slated for a cottage look shifted to bohemian as a result of vintage finds with a story. Like the rest of the elements surrounding the bed, simplicity and function fill the bill for the burden basket, which adds warmth and a sense of well-being to the bedroom. The finish on the bed is the perfect backdrop.

TOP RIGHT The hand stitching found on Kantha quilts is stunning and a key element in their intricate design.

RIGHT Old books and worn pottery carry on the reflective theme found inside these sleeping quarters. Sweet dreams!

KNOW HOW

Don't be afraid to blend store-bought items with vintage treasures.

LEFT The bed frame came back to beautiful with old-fashioned products and a little elbow grease. The fringe of the burden basket—a cool element in the room—provides the softness needed for balance.

ABOVE Vintage pillowcases are soft and comfy. Lace detailing of this quality won't be found on new linens.

TRADITION TRANSLATION

With the cornerstone pieces in place, I turned my attention to other details that would reflect the steeped-in-tradition backbone of the bedroom. My mission was to honor strong women by shaping an environment that offered sanctuary, comfort, and healing from strife and struggle. The bedding is lush and layered with an intentional combination of old and new. The colorway, inspired by the

Kantha, is both rich and restful. The furnishings are worn, yet of strong body. The burden basket is intentionally empty and prominent, reflecting rest without worry.

The place you slumber should bring comfort and renewal. My bedroom is the chosen land in my dwelling. I hope this story encourages you to invest time for thought when decorating the place you call home.

BOHEMIAN BED

Ladies and gentlemen, I have good news. When refinishing furniture, there are alternatives to paint! Here's a quick and easy fix for preserving the patina of a well-weathered metal bed. I adore the look of rust, but rust flakes on my linens—not so much! If rust is your thing, encapsulating is the key.

MATERIALS NEEDED

· Wood and Metal Finisher's Toolbox (see p. 22)

· Vintage metal full-size bed

· 4 carpet furniture sliders

TOOLS NEEDED

· Junker's Toolbox (see p. 12)

· Safety First Kit (see p. 18)

· My bed required no tools, but yours may. Removing the casters on some might only require a pair of pliers, while others call for a metal cutting tool such as a hacksaw, circular saw, or grinder.

continued on p. 158

continued from p. 157

METHOD

1. Remove the casters. My casters twisted out by hand, but yours may require tools.

2. Put on gloves. Remove dirt and loose rust particles with a shop rag or sponge and warm, soapy water. **A**

SAFETY FIRST

It's imperative that you wear gloves when cleaning rust. You don't want to get cut by the particles or allow rusty debris to get into open wounds on your hands.

3. Strap on a respirator or protective dust mask. In a well-cross-ventilated area or outdoors, apply Loctite Naval Jelly (a rust desolver) to the entire metal frame with a small paintbrush. Allow to process for 5 minutes. Then wipe off the jelly with a shop rag and warm, soapy water. Allow the surfaces to dry. **B**

4. Wearing your mask, sand the areas where you want to get down to bare metal with an abrasive sanding block. Sand the areas where you want more rust to remain with a medium-grit sanding block. **C**

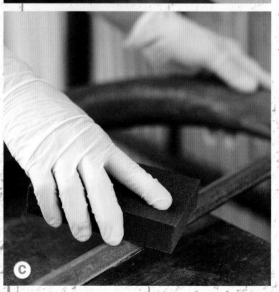

What was originally slated for a cottage look shifted to bohemian as a result of vintage finds with a story.

5. Wearing your mask and working in a well-cross-ventilated area or outdoors, apply Penetrol to all metal surfaces. **D** For best results, allow to dry for 24 hours.

6. Wearing a respirator or protective mask and working in a well-ventilated area or outdoors, spray a thin coat of clear satin polyurethane on all metal surfaces. **E** Allow to dry for 2 hours, then repeat the process 2 more times.

7. Buff the metal with a shop rag. **F** Place furniture sliders under each leg of the bed.

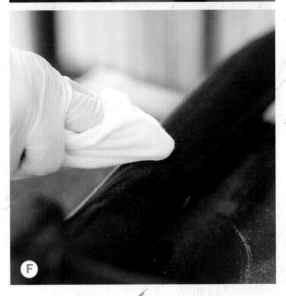

QUIET NIGHT LIFE

LUMINESCENT NIGHTLIGHT

The soft, subtle glow of a nightlight generates a feeling of calm and well-being. That's the way it should be when tucking in for the evening. Nightlights don't seem as popular these days. This to me seems like a crying shame, so I thought it was high time for a fitting reintroduction.

The white picket fence headboards and the timeless suitcase nightstand are perfect bed partners for my pearly white nightlight. The understated brown and gray tones in the room guided my accessory choices, including the fetching pheasant feathers.

This nightlight was unsightly upon discovery. No worries! If something has good bones, it can be transformed. My nightlight found a good home on the stacked suitcase nightstand. The combo of colors and textures makes this collection fabulous.

LIGHT THE WAY

I picked this up at a favorite antique mall for a mere $12. This curiosity was tucked on a bottom shelf behind many larger vintage wares. It must have been that tawdry gold and the glare from the glass block that caught my eye. I burrowed through the stuff in front and rescued the lamp. I then proceeded, as I oftentimes do, to sit on the floor and study my gem. I wanted it to remain a light fixture but was not at all sure in what form.

One of my issues was to come up with a material to line the base of the lamp that was heat resistant. While at the grocery store, I picked up parchment paper for its intended use, and that lit the way for my project. Inspiration can be found in unexpected places. Parchment paper is indeed heat resistant, and its transparent white guided my way to the overall design of the fixture. The white base lined with parchment paper and the frosted finish on the glass block are like-minded companions. The lettering is an added treat and breaks up the solidness of the etched glass.

A little romance goes a long way. The pocket watch necklace pairs nicely with the vintage alarm clock.

MAKE IT

LUMINESCENT NIGHTLIGHT

The tackiness of this midcentury TV lamp made me have to have it. I am certain that the glass block was not original to the base, but rather someone wedded the two until death do they part. It was not the best of marriages, so I challenged myself to give the couple a fighting chance.

MATERIALS NEEDED

- Painter's Toolbox (see p. 14)
- Crafter's Toolbox (see p. 24)
- Midcentury TV lamp
- Low-voltage Edison lightbulb
- White spray paint
- Armour Etch®
- Parchment paper
- 1-in. adhesive craft letters

TOOLS NEEDED

- Safety First Kit (see p. 18)
- No tools required

METHOD

1. Remove the glass block from the lamp base. Remove the red paper lining and lighting hardware from the base. **A**

2. Spray-paint the metal base with white spray paint. **B**

3. Measure the inside of the lamp base and cut the parchment paper to fit. I folded the parchment in half to diffuse the light more. Line the inside of the lamp base with the parchment and reassemble the lighting hardware. The hardware holds the parchment paper in place.

4. Apply tape and position the adhesive craft letters using the tape as your guide. **C** Remove the tape.

5. Using an art brush, apply Armour Etch to one side of the block at a time. **D** Allow it to set for the recommended time, and then rinse with water. Repeat this process until the entire glass block is completed. Remove the adhesive craft letters.

6. Insert the Edison lightbulb and put the glass block back on the lamp base.

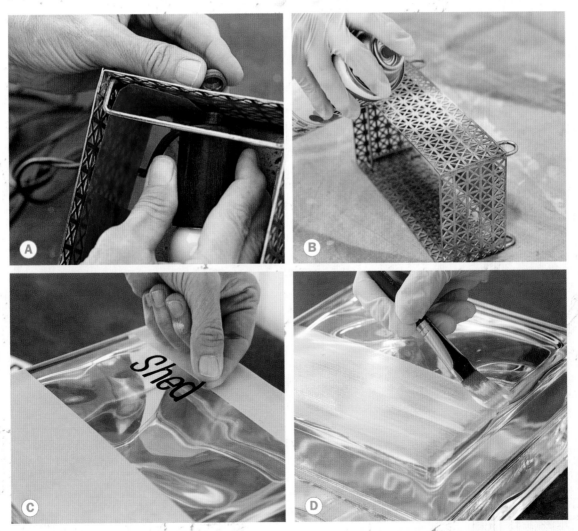

BLANKET REFUGE

ROLL-AROUND BLANKET CHEST

This chest was a must-have for many reasons. I fell for the color immediately, but when I opened it and discovered it was lined with posters of men in Speedo® swimsuits, I had to have it. Of course, I could not show that in the "before" pictures, but I can talk about it. Too funny!

EASY-PEASY FINISH

After I recovered from my belly laugh episode over the sighting of the hilarious inside lining of the chest, I began in earnest with the redesign of the disaster kit. Don't fret—I did make every attempt to preserve the integrity of the posters to be employed as comic relief at a later date. The streamlined construction emphasizing the inset handles and tight-fitting upper shelf was intriguing to me. The chest was fabricated for efficient transport to disaster sites, so it had to fit snugly into tight quarters yet preserve and protect its contents. Ingenious! This made conversion from a disaster kit to a blanket chest a bit of a breeze.

The seafoam and red color scheme was spot-on, but the paint finish had seen some action, leaving it a bit soiled and dingy. I was able to make the finish sparkle with a good cleaning, very light sanding, and a finishing protective coat. I was careful to safeguard the red lettering during this process.

FACING PAGE Much thought was put into the construction of this disaster kit transport container, making it perfect for blanket storage.

BELOW The red lettering left me with no other option than cherry red casters for legs. It was a Captain Obvious moment.

LEFT The cherry red letters are one of the chest's best features. Preserving the print was of utmost importance to me.

BELOW Repeat in design is a good thing. My overall color story is echoed in a well-cared-for vintage feed sack.

FACING PAGE The oodles of opportunity for linen storage made me a happy camper. The coordinating fabrics that line the chest and drawers wear better than paper.

KNOW HOW

Liquid starch can be difficult to find. Do some online research before you head out the door to shop.

OH, MY!!!

The exterior of the medical transport container dictated the inside alterations. Pops of color were desperately needed to add some life to the bare interior. Turning ho-hum into oh, my! was straightforward. I used a trick I've been using for years. Lightweight textiles in coordinating colors of seafoam and red were selected and adhered to the bottom of the box and drawer unit using liquid starch and a chip brush. Bam! What goes on can come off. This process does not have to be permanent, but it will hold up for as long as you like. If you tire of your fabric selection, simply peel it off and make another choice.

MAKE IT

ROLL-AROUND BLANKET CHEST

Hmm . . . a medical disaster kit for 25 patients in seafoam and red? More unusual things have been rescued, but not many. This was obviously handcrafted at some type of base. Whoever made it had a keen eye for color and design. I'm not sure the patients cared much, but I am happy to have found it!

MATERIALS NEEDED

- Wood and Metal Finisher's Toolbox (see p. 22)
- Painter's Toolbox (see p. 14)
- Crafter's Toolbox (see p. 24)
- Vintage medical disaster kit
- 4 heavy-duty 4-in. red casters
- Approximately 1 yd. of patterned seafoam fabric
- 2 fat quarters (18 in. by 22 in. each) of patterned red fabric
- 2 rolls of ½-in.-wide red grosgrain ribbon
- Liquid starch
- Spray polyurethane

TOOLS NEEDED

- Junker's Toolbox (see p. 12)
- Safety First Kit (see p. 18)

METHOD

1. Remove the content label from the inside top cover. Remove the drawer unit and any other contents. Sand the entire disaster kit with fine-grit sandpaper. I used a power hand sander, but you can also use a block.

2. Clean the disaster kit with a rag and warm, soapy water.

3. Apply paste wax to all outside surfaces and inside edges of the disaster kit, including the drawer unit.

4. Wearing a mask and working in a well-ventilated area, apply several light coats of spray polyurethane to the outside surfaces of the disaster kit. Allow to dry between coats.

5. Turn the disaster kit upside down. Place a carpenter square at each corner to locate each caster and mark a hole for each. **A** The width of the square was a perfect distance from the edge, making marking a snap. Drill holes where marked at each corner.

6. Measure and cut the seafoam fabric for the bottom of the disaster kit. Do the same with the red fabric for the drawer unit. Don't worry about getting into the edges too tightly. You'll apply ribbon over the edges later.

7. Using a chip brush, apply liquid starch to the bottom of the disaster kit. Lay the seafoam fabric on the bottom and smooth it with your fingers, working from the center out. Apply 2 more thin coats of liquid fabric starch over the fabric, allowing it to dry between coats. Repeat this process on the drawer unit with the red fabric. **B**

8. Using an X-Acto knife or box cutter, trim any excess fabric that overhangs the edges.

9. Measure and cut lengths of red ribbon for the bottom of the disaster kit and inside the drawers. Miter the ends of the ribbon by folding it at a 45-degree angle; cut with scissors. **C**

10. Adhere the ribbon to the fabric with liquid starch. Note that if your ribbon is too thick, you may need to use fabric glue instead of liquid starch.

11. Using the tip of the scissors, cut small holes through the seafoam fabric to allow bolts to come through to attach the casters. Do your best to align the holes where you think the bolts will come through. If you misplace a cut, you can add a little liquid starch to that spot of fabric once the casters are installed.

12. Flip the disaster kit over and attach the casters at all 4 corners. Tighten the bolts with a wrench and pliers. **D**

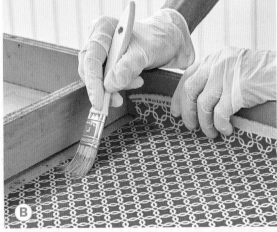

ART DECO RE-DO

ART DECO DESK

This re-do is a combination of restoration and repurpose. I didn't want to destroy the integrity of the Art Deco design, but it had a hiccup that needed to be addressed: The backsplash was falling off. I could have simply repaired it, but I wanted to give the piece greater flexibility and purpose.

PRESTO, CHANGE-O

Is it a desk or is it a vanity? The correct answer is either! You know me—if there's a viable path for me to design a piece of furniture having multiple personalities, I'll do it. I call it the Furniture Freedom Act, JUNKMARKET Style. Freedom to reposition a furnishing about the house spontaneously to fill a variety of jobs is one of my core objectives. With that said, let's focus on its life as a vanity.

The addition of a mirror was essential. Finding a vintage mirror to fit would have been my first choice. The good news is that when I do get my hands on an old mirror, I will only be out $20 for the store-bought version. The desk itself needed very little rethinking. The drawer arrangement made it a vanity natural.

RIGHT Vintage floral frogs are yet another staple in the land of junk. They are always functional and fashionable.

FACING PAGE The amalgamation of wood tones is one of the highlights of this desk, and I concluded it should be left undisturbed.

The original knobs were in mint condition. Lucky me!

The warm wood of the desk partners perfectly with the contemporary metal details on the vanity base.

I'm a sucker for details. It's nice to have curves on an otherwise straight-lined piece of furniture.

A DESK OF MANY COLORS

This piece is a chameleon in more than one way. The gorgeous natural wood of several shades and its unassuming style make it a candidate for virtually any décor. If your style leans toward modern, the vanity would be somewhat expected, but if you incorporate it in a cottage setting, it would be one of those unanticipated pleasures.

The confidence to mix styles is an acquired trait. I encourage everyone to give it a try. The worst that can happen is you make a mistake. We all know that beautiful things are born of mishaps.

The hardware on the once-upon-a-time desk backsplash now comes in handy to hold your vintage necklace collection.

LEFT AND ABOVE A fresh herbal bouquet in a vintage Mason jar is a refreshing alternative to predictable flowers on a bedroom vanity.

LEFT The drawers will house everything a girl needs for grooming. I like to line drawers with vintage linens, but you also can utilize store-bought containers (don't forget to line with vintage linens!) for easy in-and-out access.

The confidence to mix styles is an acquired trait. I encourage everyone to give it a try.

KNOW HOW

Know your stuff! If you are unsure of whether you should paint a piece or restore it to its original state, it's best to do your research on overall value before making a decision.

MAKE IT

ART DECO DESK

For all of you lovers of Art Deco, this one's for you—it's a beauty! It was a little broken and a wee bit rough around the edges when I brought it home, but not to worry. A little creative thought and use of good product goes a long way when refashioning vintage furniture.

MATERIALS NEEDED

- Wood and Metal Finisher's Toolbox (see p. 22)
- Vintage Art Deco desk
- Mirror, 24 in. by 30 in.
- Hickory color gel stain
- Mahogany color gel stain
- Antique maple color gel stain
- 4 mirror clips

TOOLS NEEDED

- Junker's Toolbox (see p. 12)
- Safety First Kit (see p. 18)

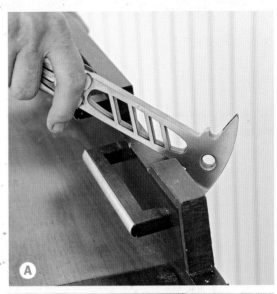

METHOD

1. Using a hammer, gently tap loose and remove the backsplash of the desk. Remove any nails as well. **A**

2. Wearing a mask and gloves, clean the desk, the backsplash you removed, and the inside of the drawers with Sunnyside TSP Substitute. Wipe them down with a rag and warm water, then wipe dry.

3. Lightly hand-sand the outside wood surfaces with fine-grit sandpaper. (You might also need to sand inside the drawers if they are beat up. Mine weren't.) **B** Wipe down all surfaces with a tack cloth.

4. Apply gel stain to the desk, starting with 1 coat of hickory stain on the darkest wood, followed by 1 coat of mahogany stain on the medium-color wood, and 1 coat of antique maple stain on the lightest wood. Let each color dry before applying the next. **C**

continued on p. 176

continued from p. 175

5. Apply a coat of Howard Feed-N-Wax with a clean rag; don't forget the back piece. Wipe away the extra and buff with a dusting mitt. **D**

6. Clean and polish all metal with a solution of 1 part water to 1 part vinegar.

7. Attach the backsplash of the desk to the mirror with epoxy, then clamp until dry. **E** Be cautious when attaching the mirror to the backsplash. Clamp lightly to allow the epoxy to dry without cracking the mirror. A block of wood and/or cloth could be used in the clamping process to help avoid cracking the mirror.

8. Measure and mark for hanging screws on the back of the backsplash. Predrill where marked, then screw in screws partway. Wrap picture hanging wire around each screw and then tighten. Hang the mirror over the vanity, securing it to the wall with 2 mirror clips on either side.

A little creative thought and use of good product goes a long way when refashioning vintage furniture.

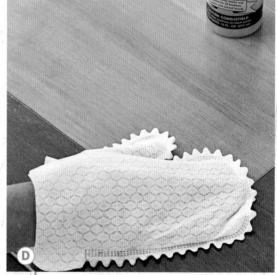

RETREAT AND RESTORE

MAKEOVERS FOR GETAWAY SPACES

The job, the kids, the chores, and other everyday responsibilities can leave a junker begging for mercy. A safe haven where we can work without distraction, successfully enjoy a parent's time-out, or simply kick back and relax in heavenly solitude may seem like it's too good to be true. Not to worry! A few sleight-of-hand furniture re-dos combined with some reasonable and enforceable quiet time rules can help establish a state-of-grace getaway. A library, a reading nook, or a hallway hideaway are just a few spaces where you can retreat without upsetting the family apple cart.

TABLE ON THE MOVE

ROLL-ABOUT DESK

Versatility is the name of the game when it comes to home furnishings. A piece that can move about the cabin freely is surely welcome in any abode. I was thrilled to uncover this amazing and utilitarian vintage adjustable table, like those used for hospital bed trays. Its many practical uses will boggle your junker's mind!

FACING PAGE This table of many functions can move from room to room and address a multitude of household needs. True story!

BELOW LEFT Whoa, Nellie! Please don't remove the label. Trademarks with patent dates are informational and oh-so-amazing.

BELOW RIGHT The handle used to adjust the table is both functional and decorative.

TABLETOP TRANSFORMER

My table on the move is indeed a home furnishing with some athletic prowess. I might refer to it as a CrossFit® enthusiast or even quite possibly a Tough Mudder. I play a game with myself every time I discover a new diamond in the rough. My challenge is to come up with as many plausible and practical everyday uses as possible for my project in waiting. I have found through many years of experience that the more adaptable a furnishing is, the less likely you are to grow weary of it.

This Sidway adjustable table boasts more than the average number of chameleon characteristics. I have revealed several interpretations of this multitasker in a library, but it would feel just as at home in a bathroom as a bath tray, over your bed as a reading table, or in the kitchen as a cookbook holder. Come on, table—get to work. Stand up, sit down, and fight, fight, fight! I was a cheerleader in high school. Who knew?

BELOW This desk is spring loaded and ready to handle anything you throw on it. The original mechanism still works.

BELOW LEFT A state-of-the-art desk such as this deserves a beautiful setting. A traditional backdrop like this one softens the hard lines of the desk.

KNOW HOW

Styling your home is as important as each individual furniture piece. Step out of your comfort zone and create a look that's unique and unanticipated.

EVERY DAY UPS AND DOWNS

Active and *fit* are two words constantly on our minds these days. The onset of the Fitbit® and other such devices relentlessly keeps us aware of our physical movements. The desk, in its standing position, will help you get in those extra steps needed to achieve your daily goal and receive your reward sticker. However, there are moments when no one is watching and we want to sneak in a little unwinding time.

This adaptable desk can do that for you, too. Just crank down the height, pull up a chair, and enjoy. No worries! Your secret is safe with me. Finding a good home for your desk is a key ingredient. A library bookcase dolled up with a delightful combination of vintage wares sets the stage in style.

BELOW LEFT Active people want a desk that keeps them up, moving about, and off their backsides. Beware! Your Fitbit is watching.

BELOW RIGHT After a hard day at the office, one deserves time alone with the paper and a martini, right?

MAKE IT

ROLL-ABOUT DESK

Pieces that can be used for different purposes are worth their weight in gold. This hospital table is one of those finds. It can move from room to room in your home and can handle a multitude of chores. What's not to love?

MATERIALS NEEDED

· Wood and Metal Finisher's Toolbox (see p. 22)
· Vintage adjustable table
· Gray-tinted primer
· Black gloss latex paint

TOOLS NEEDED

· Junker's Toolbox (see p. 12)
· Safety First Kit (see p. 18)

METHOD

1. Remove all veneer from the bottom of the hospital table with a putty knife. **A**

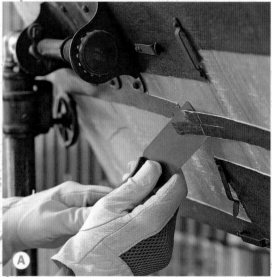

2. Wearing gloves and a mask, clean the wood with Sunnyside TSP Substitute; then clean the wood and metal with a rag and warm, soapy water.

3. Using your putty knife, apply wood filler to the top of the table to repair any damaged veneer. **B** After the filler is dry, sand the top gently with fine-grit sandpaper to smooth the surface. Also sand the bottom of the tabletop. Remove sanding residue with a tack cloth.

4. Wearing your mask and gloves and working in a well-cross-ventilated area, brush Penetrol onto the metal stand. **C**

5. Wearing a safety mask and gloves and working in a well-ventilated area, apply several coats of spray polyurethane. Allow dry time between each coat. **D**

6. Using a roller, apply several light coats of a gray-tinted primer to the top and sides of the table. Allow the primer to dry between coats.

7. Using a roller, paint the tabletop in very light coats with the black latex paint. Allow the paint to dry between coats. You'll probably need 4 or 5 coats of paint. **E**

8. Brush Minwax Polycrylic onto the tabletop and sides. **F**

9. Using a staining pad, stain the bottom of the tabletop.

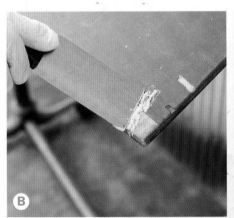

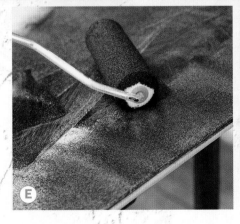

EAMES IMPERSONATION

MODERN DESK CHAIR

Wowsers! Now this is what I call a critical conversion. I learned through the makeover process that the previous painter of this chair was certainly committed to his mission! I'm not saying it was the best choice, but I applaud the effort that went into it. I am here to tell you that it was quite the chore to remove the hideous paint. Patience, elbow grease, and the appropriate product and tools restored the chair's integrity.

MODERN AND REFINED

I now adore this roadside recovery, as it resembles an Eames molded plywood lounge chair. The "Eames look," which was introduced in the 1940s, is sleek, modern, functional, and delightfully simple. The only thing better than owning this timeless treasure would be to own the real deal.

A modern chair meets old-world piano stool. Unlikely pairing, but it so works!

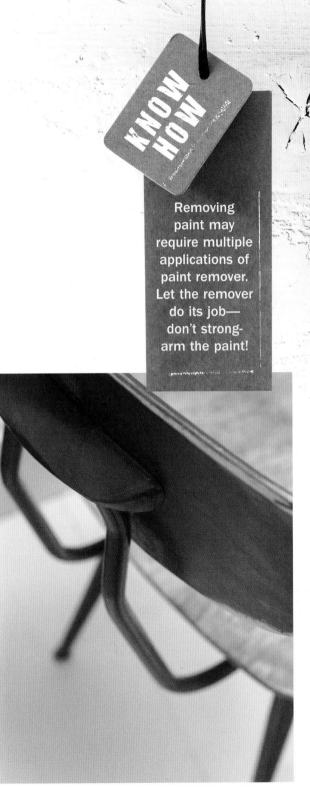

KNOW HOW

Removing paint may require multiple applications of paint remover. Let the remover do its job— don't strong-arm the paint!

ABOVE Paintbrushes don't have to be vintage to register on the awesome meter. Recycle them as modern-day art.

RIGHT Automotive paint rendered the metal sleek, shiny, and like brand new again!

BELOW A plain Jane pitcher and an antler together become the perfect complement to this nook-and-cranny duo.

MAKE IT

MODERN DESK CHAIR

This is an ugly duckling transformation. I love making something beautiful when it appears there is no hope. With a little time and some elbow grease, the dreadful blue and yellow paint disappeared, leaving a clean slate with which to work. A combo of stain and paint put this chair back to its intended appearance.

MATERIALS NEEDED

· Wood and Metal Finisher's Toolbox (see p. 22)
· Painter's Toolbox (see p. 14)
· Vintage desk chair
· Automotive paint prep wipe
· Gray-tinted primer
· Black gloss latex paint
· Dark brown gel stain

TOOLS NEEDED

· Junker's Toolbox (see p. 12)
· Safety First Kit (see p. 18)

METHOD

1. Brush or wipe paint remover onto all painted surfaces. The paint will be ready to scrape off when it changes color (about 15 or 20 minutes). Scrape off the paint with a putty knife. **A** Repeat the process as needed.

2. Sand the entire chair (metal and wood) with fine- to medium-grit sandpaper, then remove the residue with a tack cloth.

3. Clean the metal on the chair and the metal legs with an automotive paint prep wipe. **B**

4. With painter's tape, tape the chair in preparation for spraying. You'll need to tape off right around the metal areas you'll be spraying.

5. Wearing a respirator or safety mask and working in a well-ventilated area, preferably outside, spray the metal legs and back with automotive spray paint. **C**

6. Let the metal dry following the manufacturer's instructions, then prime the entire chair back with gray-tinted primer. **D** Once dry, paint the chair back with black paint. Once the paint is dry, sand the chair back to create a look that is antiqued.

7. Using a shop rag, apply special dark paste wax to the entire chair, then buff. **E**

8. Stain the seat with dark brown gel stain. Let dry. Wearing a respirator or protective mask and working in a well-ventilated area, apply polyurethane to the entire chair.

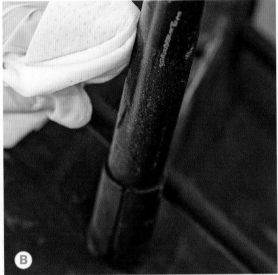

LEATHER AND LACE REVIVAL

VELVETEEN CHAIR REBORN

This awe-inspiring transformation was fashioned in honor of one of my all-time favorite songs and two of my favorite artists: "Leather and Lace" by the one and only Stevie Nicks and her cohort in creation, the Eagles' Don Henley. Like Don, this chair won't be walking out your door. Promise!

PURE AND SIMPLE REHAB

I giggle a bit when reflecting upon this chair's humble beginnings. I'm not sure what drew me to the piece. I'm not a girly girl, I'm not really into crushed velvet, and quite frankly, I've never been partial to ruffles. I'm not suggesting that any of these characteristics are bad, but rather acknowledging that this particular chair presented a challenge for me. Thus, the labor of love began. The first thing to go was the ruffle. No surprise there! The ruffle removal exposed simple legs with clean lines that I instantly knew would aid in the transformation from tawdry to chaste.

Painting textiles is an undertaking, but the results are well worth your time. I have found that when tackling textiles, chalked paint is your best bet. When clear wax is applied properly, sanded, and finished after painting, the velveteen takes on a well-worn leather look and feel. Nice! Before crossing the finish line, the chair legs were painted and lightly distressed. I refined the bottom of the chair with ethereal white lace.

FACING PAGE Through a labor of love, this chair was transformed from a foul blue goose into a striking swan of white.

RIGHT I'm a sucker for anything vintage, but I do have my favorites. Vintage paper and glasses—they make the cut.

MAMA, TAKE A SEAT

My children may be grown, but I remember the times when all I needed was a wee bitty break in the action. Back in the day, I lovingly referred to those moments as Mom's time-out. The kiddies were never too thrilled about them, but hey, sometimes a girl's got to do what a girl's got to do! Could this memory be my attraction to this chair? I think maybe so.

As you already know, the blue velveteen and ruffle were not speaking my language. I did, however, recognize the potential in this little lovely and identified it as a ready and willing contender for a chalked-paint restoration. Once completed, the dainty ditty found a new hideaway home tucked under a staircase as a rest and relaxation station.

ABOVE This piece was desperate for delicate detail. Store-bought white lace and hem tape came to the rescue.

LEFT Flowers spring into action with an upcycled olive oil bottle and a vintage spring.

KNOW HOW

Be a savvy shopper. Choose value and quality when selecting paint. More expensive does not always mean better.

VELVETEEN CHAIR REBORN

Can you believe the change in this chair? If you didn't know any better, you would think the original and the reborn were two separate pieces. It's amazing what a little chalked paint will do! Apply the paint in thin layers, giving it time to absorb between coats. This will transform the velveteen to a beautiful leather-like finish.

MATERIALS NEEDED

- Wood and Metal Finisher's Toolbox (see p. 22)
- Crafter's Toolbox (see p. 24)
- Rust-Oleum Chalked Paint in Linen White
- Light gray satin latex paint

TOOLS NEEDED

- Junker's Toolbox (see p. 12)
- Safety First Kit (see p. 18)

METHOD

1. Using a craft knife, remove the ruffle from the chair. **A**

2. Sand the legs with a fine- to medium-grit sanding block or sandpaper. Wipe off the sanding residue with a tack cloth, then apply primer to the chair legs. When dry, paint the legs with light gray latex paint.

continued on p. 192

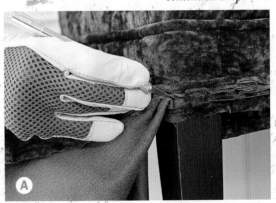

A

continued from p. 191

3. Thin the chalk paint with water, approximately 3 parts paint to 1 part water. Depending on the fabric, you may wish to alter the formula. **B**

4. Brush on a light coat of chalked paint, covering the velveteen. Let dry. Apply several more light coats, letting each dry before applying the next. **C**

5. Sand the painted fabric with a fine-grit sanding block or sandpaper. **D** Using a clean rag, apply a light coat of soft wax on the fabric. Let it dry thoroughly. The wax should soften the paint so the fabric feels like leather. If it doesn't, add another coat of wax.

6. Distress the legs with a fine-grit sanding block or sandpaper. **E** Wipe off the sanding residue with a tack cloth, then apply paste wax to the legs.

7. Measure around the bottom of the chair, adding about 2 in. extra, then cut a length of lace to that measurement. Glue, then tack the lace to the chair. **F**

8. Glue hem tape over the top of the lace where glued to the chair. **G**

RIVETED ON RATTAN

REFRESHED RATTAN PATIO SET

The ultimate getaway for the whole family is undeniably the porch. Porches come in all shapes and sizes. Regardless of the style of your quarters, a vintage rattan patio collection will feel right at home. Dress it up with a thoughtful combination of vintage and new tableware, and you'll be set!

FOR THE LOVE OF RATTAN

I was beyond tickled pink when I spotted this outdoor patio masterpiece. It is rare to find a complete set of this variety in working order and good repair. I was immediately drawn to the clean modern design, so I bought it on the spot, took it home, and started my research. Telescope Casual Furniture company produced the grouping and is a well-respected outdoor furniture manufacturer that has been in business since 1903. I was fascinated to find that the company actually has archived catalogs online as far back as 1927. As luck would have it, I was able to get the skinny on this exact set in the Telescope Casual catalog from 1960. How cool is that?

The furniture is constructed from imported rattan, hardwood, and aluminum. Conveniently, each piece in the set folds up neatly so that it can be stored easily when not in use. Needless to say, I felt like I had won the lottery when I uncovered this beauty!

TOP LEFT By pure chance, I discovered that average 16-in. by 16-in. throw pillows fit the chair seats to a T.

LEFT Labels assist in research. Who knows—you may discover you've purchased an item of far greater value than you originally thought.

PERFECT IMPERFECTIONS

Some found treasures can be altered without harming the value, while others are best either left alone or restored to their original splendor. The Telescope Casual furnishings were suitable for restoration. I officially put this set on the do-not-paint list! A few minor bumps and bruises were taken care of by using proper cleaning techniques, removing broken rattan, and gluing loose pieces back into place. Sanding and refinishing of the hardwood was also necessary. Some of the hardwood was more damaged in places than others, and not all could be brought back to its showroom condition.

Working with vintage pieces is not like crafting with new materials. Many times, a few imperfections will persist. In my world, we refer to that as character, or perfect imperfection.

KNOW HOW

This furniture set has endured well, as it is crafted from rattan that is a sturdier material than others used in the wicker-weaving process.

FACING PAGE The contemporary tailoring of this vintage rattan furniture is the picture-perfect accompaniment for a bright and cheery front porch. Adorable!

BELOW LEFT AND RIGHT Mixing vintage and new dinnerware is totally acceptable and practical to boot.

Many times, a few imperfections will persist. In my world, we refer to that as character, or perfect imperfection.

The umbrella hole has been cleverly hidden by a vintage lazy Susan. A vintage jar filled with goodies accents the charming coffee pot with its sleek wooden handle.

REFRESHED RATTAN PATIO SET

This set is amazing just as it is, so hold the paintbrushes. All that is needed for a suite like this is a little repair work and a good old-fashioned cleaning! Take your time, and make sure to fix all of the broken rattan pieces to give your table and chairs a longer life.

KNOW HOW

Vinegar and water are best friends when it comes to a cleaning solution. It makes a green and natural cleaner. Mix a solution of equal parts.

MATERIALS NEEDED

- Wood and Metal Finisher's Toolbox (see p. 22)
- Painter's Toolbox (see p. 14)
- Rattan patio set (table and chairs)
- Toothbrush
- Antique maple gel stain

TOOLS NEEDED

- Junker's Toolbox (see p. 12)
- Safety First Kit (see p. 18)

continued on p. 198

continued from p. 197

METHOD

1. Remove or repair any broken rattan with wood glue, then clamp and let dry. **A**

2. Clean the rattan with a vinegar solution of 1 part vinegar to 1 part warm water and a toothbrush. **B**

3. Wearing gloves and a mask, clean the wood with Sunnyside TSP Substitute and wash with a rag and warm, soapy water.

4. Sand the wood with a fine- to medium-grit sandpaper or block. If you like, use a power disk sander, but be careful not to over sand. **C** Remove residue with a tack cloth.

5. Apply gel stain to the wood and let dry. **D**

6. Using a brush, apply Minwax Polycrylic to the wood and let dry. **E**

7. Using a rag, clean and polish the aluminum with a vinegar solution of 1 part vinegar to 1 part warm water. **F**

RESOURCES

ADOURN
218 Main St. S.
Chatfield, MN 55923
(507) 251-4202
https://www.facebook.com/
Adourn-110611008958318/

BEAUTIFUL SOMETHING
106 Coffee St.
Lanesboro, MN 55949
(507) 271-6638
https://www.facebook.com/
beautifulsomethinglanesboromn/

BLACK CROW GALLERY
110 Coffee St. E.
Lanesboro, MN 55949
(563) 419-0727

CHERYLS FABRIC GARDEN/HANDCRAFTED BOUTIQUE
108 Coffee St. E.
Lanesboro, MN 55949
(507) 467-4466
https://www.cherylsfabricgarden.com

COTTAGE ELEMENTS
http://www.cottageelements.com

E2 BOUTIQUE
115 Parkway Ave. N.
Lanesboro, MN 55949
(507) 467-2994
https://www.facebook.com/WomensChildrensClothing/

EMMA'S NOOK & GRANNY
https://www.facebook.com/pages/
Emmas-Nook-Granny/146365712145794?pnref=lhc
https://www.facebook.com/marge.utley?fref=ts

FOUR DAUGHTERS VINEYARD & WINERY
78757 State Highway 16
Spring Valley, MN 55975
(507) 346-7300
http://www.fourdaughtersvineyard.com
https://www.facebook.com/4daughterswine/

GRANNY'S LIQUOR
113 Parkway Ave. N.
Lanesboro, MN, 55949
(507) 467-2700
https://www.facebook.com/GrannysLiquor/

JOYFUL REVIVAL
41001 565th St.
Mazeppa, MN 55956
(507) 358-9042
https://www.facebook.com/pg/joyfulrevival/
about/?ref=page_internal

JUNK REDEFINED BY THE PFARKEL SISTERS
29452 County 11
Fountain, MN 55935
(507) 250-1690
https://www.facebook.com/pg/Junk-redefined-
by-the-Pfarkel-Sisters-223786781095648/
about/?ref=page_internal

NAOMIS TIN TREASURES
https://www.etsy.com/shop/NaomisTinTreasures

NEW GENERATIONS OF HARMONY ANTIQUE MALL
50 Industrial Blvd. NE
Harmony, MN 55939
(507) 886-6660
http://generationsofharmony.com
https://www.facebook.com/generationsofharmony/

PARKWAY MARKET AND COFFEE HOUSE
201 Parkway Ave. N.
Lanesboro, MN 55949
(507) 467-2500
https://www.facebook.com/lanesborogrocery/

REFIND WORKS
(507) 438-1436
https://www.facebook.com/pg/refindworks/
about/?ref=page_internal

TADA! CONSIGN
1814 2nd St. SW
Rochester, MN 55902
(507) 280-9307
http://www.tadaconsign.com/about-us/
https://www.facebook.com/
TaDa-Consign-1685330158392159/

UNTAINTED SKIN CARE
422 Second St.
Excelsior, MN 55331
(763) 232-5855
http://www.untaintedskincare.com

INDEX

A

Antique malls, 10–11
Antique white, 21
Architectural salvage, 2–3, 88–93
Art shows, 11

B

Barn-board tabletop, 26–29
Barn sales, 11
Baskets
	Cherokee burden basket, 155, 156
	wicker basket, 148–51
Bathroom projects, 101–15
	Crafty Curio Conversion, 102–7
	Ladderback Chair Bathroom Caddy, 112–15
	Rustic Towel Bar, 108–11
Bedroom projects, 152–76
	Art Deco Desk, 170–76
	Bohemian Bed, 153–59
	Luminescent Nightlight, 160–63
	Roll-around Blanket Chest, 164–69
Beds
	Bohemian Bed, 153–59
	picket fence headboards, 160
Bench
	Child's Bench, 50–54
Birch bark preservation tip, 109
Blanket chest, 164–69
Blanket holder, 137–41
Boot Tray, 46–49
Buttery white, 21

C

Carhop caddy, 130–35
Chairs
	Modern Desk Chair, 184–87
	Modern Dining Table and Chairs, 81–87
	Refreshed Rattan Patio Set, 193–98
	Velveteen Chair Reborn, 188–92
Chalk-based paint, 15, 188, 190–92
Chalkboard and Easel, 70–75
Cherokee burden basket, 155, 156
Chick transporter, 46–49
Cleaning solution, 197

Crackle glaze, 94–100
Crafter's Toolbox, 24–25
Curio cabinet, 102–7

D

Design
	role of humor in, 130
	three P rule, 2
Desks
	Art Deco Desk, 170–76
	Roll-about Desk, 178–83
Destruction reproduction, 51
Dining room projects, 80–100
	Architectural Salad Server, 88–93
	Intentional Crackle Glaze Sideboard, 94–100
	Modern Dining Table and Chairs, 81–87
Doorknobs, 108–11
Drapery hooks, 130, 132, 135

E

Eames chairs, 184
Easel and Chalkboard, 70–75
Eggshell (satin) latex, 16
Entryway projects, 40–54
	Boot Tray, 46–49
	Child's Bench, 50–54
	Stuff Coat Hanger, 41–45
Etsy, 3

F

File cabinet, 30–33
Flat (matte) latex, 16
Flatware box, 62–69
Flea markets, 10
Furniture Freedom Act, 170

G

Gathering room projects, 116–35
	DeWalt Game Table, 117–23
	Ladder Bar, 130–35
	Modern Coffee Table, 124–29
Getaway spaces pieces, 177–98
	Modern Desk Chair, 184–87
	Refreshed Rattan Patio Set, 193–98
	Roll-about Desk, 178–83
	Velveteen Chair Reborn, 188–92

Glass blocks, 160–63
Gloss latex, 17
Grayed-down white, 20

H

Herb garden, 76–79
Hospital table, 178–83
Humor, role of in design, 130

I

Iron bed, 153–59

J

Junker's Toolbox, 12–13
JUNKMARKET, 7

K

Kantha quilts, 154–56
Kitchen projects, 55–79
	Chalkboard and Easel, 70–75
	Flatware Box–Cum–Charging Station, 62–69
	Kitchen Window Herb Garden, 76–79
	White Breakfast Table, 56–61
Kitchen Window Herb Garden, 76–79

L

Labels, information on and tip to not remove, 118, 178, 193
Ladderback chair, 112–15
Ladder Bar, 130–35
Lampshades, 76–79
Latex paint, 15–18
	flat (matte), 16
	gloss, 17
	satin (eggshell), 16
	semi-gloss, 17
Lead paint safety, 90, 139
Letters, composite, 41–45
Lighting
	Luminescent Nightlight, 160–63
Living room projects, 136–51
	Medical Stand Blanket Holder, 137–41
	Room Divider, 142–47
	Wicker Basket Table, 148–51

M

Matte (flat) latex, 16
Medical disaster kit container, 164–69
Medical instrument stand, 137–41
Mercury glass finish, 104, 105, 107
Metal, tip for preserving patina on, 157–59
Metal and Wood Finisher's Toolbox, 22–23
Milk paint, 15, 51, 54

O

Occasional sales, 11
Oil-based paint, 18
Organ pipes, 34–37

P

Paint
    chalk-based paint, 15, 188, 190–92
    crackle glaze, 94–100
    latex paint, 15–18
    lead paint safety, 90, 139
    milk paint, 15, 51, 54
    oil-based paint, 18
    types and finishes, 15–18
    white paint, 19–21
Painter's Toolbox, 14–15
Painting or restoring a piece, decision about, 173
Parchment paper, 161–63
Patina on metal, tip for preserving, 157–59
Pinterest, 3
Pipe hangers, 108–11
Pipe projects
    Room Divider, 142–47
Polyurethane, 16, 17, 46, 90, 109, 139
Potato sorter conveyor belts, 142–47
Pure white, 20

R

Rattan patio set, 193–98
Restoring or painting a piece, decision about, 173
Retail display unit, 56–61
Room Divider, 142–47

S

Safety and Safety First Kit, 18
Sales, 11
Salvage and vintage items
    destruction reproduction, 51
    keeping in plain sight while deciding what to do with it, 124
    repurposing of, 2–5, 7
    restoring or painting, decision about, 173
    shopping for and sources for, 2, 3, 10–11
    surge of interest in, 2–3, 10
Satin (eggshell) latex, 16
Semi-gloss latex, 17
Serving pieces
    Architectural Salad Server, 88–93
    Intentional Crackle Glaze Sideboard, 94–100
    Ladder Bar, 130–35
Stain, 18
Starch, liquid, 166, 169
Stenciling, 59, 60–61
Storage and organizers
    Boot Tray, 46–49
    Crafty Curio Conversion, 102–7
    Flatware Box–Cum–Charging Station, 62–69
    Intentional Crackle Glaze Sideboard, 94–100
    Ladderback Chair Bathroom Caddy, 112–15
    Medical Stand Blanket Holder, 137–41
    Organ Pipe Art Supply Shelf, 34–37
    Paint-by-Numbers Storage, 30–33
    Roll-around Blanket Chest, 164–69
    Rustic Towel Bar and shelf, 108–11
    Stuff Coat Hanger, 41–45
    Tool Time Caddy, 26–29

T

Tables
    DeWalt Game Table, 117–23
    Modern Coffee Table, 124–29
    Modern Dining Table and Chairs, 81–87
    Refreshed Rattan Patio Set, 193–98
    White Breakfast Table, 56–61
    Wicker Basket Table, 148–51
Tablesaw base, 117–23
Textiles
    chalked paint for, 188, 190–92
    fabric protector for, 50
    replacing fabric and batting on bench, 52–53
TinkerToy time, 132
Toolboxes
    Crafter's Toolbox, 24–25
    Junker's Toolbox, 12–13
    Painter's Toolbox, 14–15
    Wood and Metal Finisher's Toolbox, 22–23
Towel bar
    Rustic Towel Bar, 108–11
Trailer hitch ball, 139, 141
Tree cookies, 76, 79, 149, 150–51
Typewriter roll, 132, 133, 135

V

Vanity, 170–76
Vintage and art shows, 11

W

West End Architectural Salvage, 2–3
West End Salvage, 2
White paint, 19–21
    antique white, 21
    buttery white, 21
    grayed-down white, 20
    pure white, 20
Wicker basket, 148–51
Wood
    birch bark preservation tip, 109
    composite compared to real, 43
    surplus lumber, 108–11
    wood veneer repairs, 82, 83
Wood and Metal Finisher's Toolbox, 22–23

Y

Yardstick, 47

If you like this book, you'll *love* these other titles by Sue Whitney.

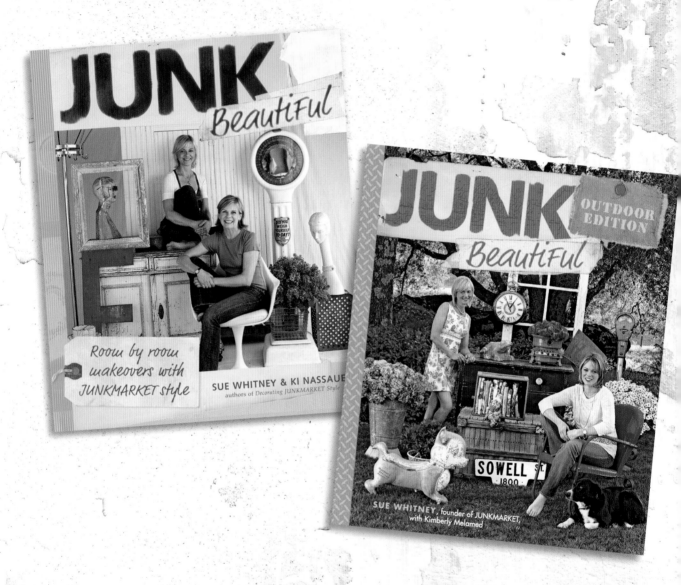

Look for these books and other Taunton Press titles wherever books are sold.